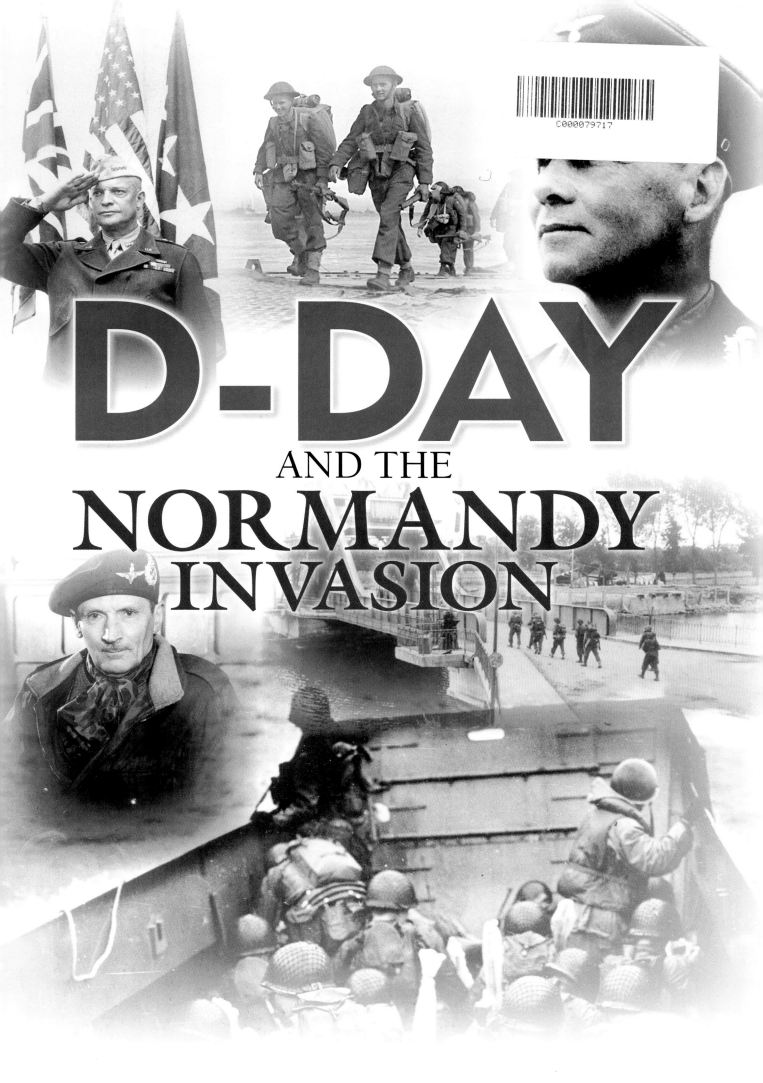

D-DAY
AND THE
NORMANDY
INVASION

Contents

2

D-DAY AND THE NORMANDY INVASION

First published in the UK in 2013

© Instinctive Product Development 2013

This edition published by Park Lane Books

www.parklanebooksltd.vpweb.co.uk

Printed in China

ISBN: 978-1-906969-31-8

Designed by: BrainWave

Creative Director: Kevin Gardner

Written by: Adam Powley

Images courtesy of PA Photos and Wiki Commons

Chapter One:
The Build-up to Battle
Summer **1940** – July **1943**

"I ask you: Do you want total war? If necessary, do you want a war more total and radical than anything that we can even yet imagine?... Now, comrades, rise up, and let the storm break loose!"

■ **ABOVE: Hitler's propaganda chief, Joseph Goebbels, standing right, during his address to German newspaper editors in Berlin, 1943.**

In February 1943, Joseph Goebbels, Adolf Hitler's propaganda chief and one of the most committed of all Nazis, gave a speech designed to stiffen German resolve. His call for total war came at a time when the Third Reich was confronted by a series of mounting threats in the aftermath of a number of strategic setbacks.

In North Africa, the twin assault of the British and the Americans was pushing the Afrika Korps to the brink of defeat and removal from the continent; Germany's ally, Italy, was on the point of military collapse, exposing a southern route to attack the German Fatherland; in the Far East, the Americans were turning the tide of battle against the Japanese.

On the Eastern Front, the Red Army was now proving that the Wehrmacht, that had wreaked such terrible devastation on its seemingly unstoppable path to the edge of Asia, could not just be beaten, but annihilated. The complete capitulation of the German 6th Army at Stalingrad had ended with the capture of nearly 100,000 utterly defeated troops, including the commanding officer, Field Marshal von Paulus. The Nazi war machine was fallible, after all.

It had seemed so different almost three years before. In the summer of 1940, the Third Reich was poised to assume complete victory and total control across Europe. Poland, Czechoslovakia, the Netherlands, Belgium, and even France had all fallen, seemingly unable to resist the Nazi war machine and its frighteningly effective tactic of *blitzkrieg* or "lightning war."

Superbly equipped and expertly led and manned by professional, well-trained personnel, German forces either reduced their opponents to a shell-shocked fleeing rabble, or simply bypassed them to render their defensive positions utterly useless. Western Europe fell in just six weeks.

As for the British army, which had crossed the English Channel expecting to hold back the German advance and end the war before it had even got properly started, the defeat was one of the most abject in the island nation's history. Undermanned, under equipped, and by comparison poorly trained and led, the ragtag of British divisions were sent desperately scampering to the coast at Dunkirk. While over 300,000 men were rescued to fight another day, the defeat had rendered British land forces largely removed from the conflict.

All that stood between Hitler and total triumph in the West was victory in the air. His plan was to call on the Luftwaffe to defeat the RAF, a body staffed by brave pilots flying some of the most advanced planes of the time, but hopelessly outnumbered. Once the Luftwaffe had gained air superiority, Britain would be invaded and the European war effectively ended. Hitler would then be able to turn his vast and powerful armed forces eastward to focus their objectives on Russia, with the ultimate aim of defeating the Soviet Union, subjugating its peoples, and casting a new world order.

History took a different turn, however, with the remarkable victory of the RAF in the Battle of Britain. Invigorated by the new Prime Minister, Winston Churchill, who took office on May 12, 1940, British, Commonwealth, and other pilots from around the world who had rallied to the anti-Nazi cause, were able to see off the Luftwaffe's fighter and bomber units. On the ground, despite months of terrible bombing that resulted in the death of 43,000 civilians, morale was battered but unbroken. Britain had survived and held firm – just – but in holding back the previously inexorable tide of German military success, the course of the war was altered.

"Democracy is finished in England," said Joseph Kennedy, the American ambassador, in November 1940. The father of future president

■ **BELOW: A German Wehrmacht soldier sits in despair on the remains of an artillery piece in the wake of the Battle of Kursk on the Eastern Front. The failure of their Operation Citadel offensive entailed massive losses in men and machinery for the Germans.**

John F. Kennedy was mistaken. For while there was considerable opposition across the Atlantic to the USA being dragged into the war, there was also a growing sense that Americans regarded the prospect of actively taking part in the conflict as inevitable. Britain's resistance won many hearts and minds, and the media played a key role. Ed Murrow's dispatches from the capital had a telling effect on public opinion. "This... is London," Murrow would announce, his gripping on-the-spot reports to a backdrop of explosions

■ **ABOVE: Ford Island: A photograph taken from a Japanese aircraft showing the Japanese surprise attack on the US Navy's Pacific Fleet in progress at Pearl Harbor, Hawaii.**

and sirens bringing the reality of what was going on in Europe into American homes, strengthening the sense of purpose that Hitler had to be defeated – and that America would have to join the fight.

It was to be a devastating experience altogether closer to home that decided the US's fate, however. Carrier-borne Japanese aircraft launched a surprise and murderous attack on the American naval base of Pearl Harbor on December 7, 1941 – a "date which will live in infamy," in the immortal words of President

with the Axis powers now confronted by the Allies across the globe, the war had taken a decisive new course.

Germany and her allies would continue to gain victories in the various theaters of war for some time yet, however. While America rearmed, the Nazis had invaded the Soviet Union in June 1941, shattering the illusion of the pact that existed between the two ideologically opposed powers; Hitler's plan for carving out an "Aryan Empire" in the East seemed a genuine and terrifying prospect. A weakened and overstretched Britain lost territory in the Far East, suffered punishing losses to her merchant fleet in the Atlantic, and clung on desperately in North Africa in a see-sawing fight to safeguard the vital Suez Canal. And in the summer of 1941, Germany began implementing the "final solution" – the wholesale genocide of entire races – in earnest. It wasn't just civilization that was at stake: it was human existence.

But within a year and a half, by the time Goebbels made his hysterical call to arms, fortunes had turned in the Allies' favor. As the Soviets rolled back the Panzer armies in Russia, the Ukraine, and elsewhere, Britain learned from its mistakes and took the fight to the German enemy. The US, calling on its vast industrial might, was making headway in Europe and pushing back the Japanese island by island in the Pacific, albeit at considerable human cost. Italy capitulated and was invaded by British and American forces. Victory had not yet been grasped, but the Allies were winning the total war.

Franklin D. Roosevelt – sinking four battleships and numerous other vessels and installations, with the loss of 2,402 lives.

The attack propelled the US into the conflict. Within a day, America had declared war on Japan; three days later the US was pitted against Germany and Italy. Addressing Congress on December 8, Roosevelt intoned that "the American people in their righteous might, will win through to absolute victory." That victory would take four long, hard, and often horrific, years to realize, but

■ ABOVE: **The USS *West Virginia* blazes after the Japanese attack at Pearl Harbor.**

Chapter Two:
The Long-term Planning

Summer **1943** – November **1943**

■ **BELOW: Russian soldiers inspect a German tank captured in the Orel-Kursk sector, Russia.**

Once Germany had invaded the Soviet Union and the illusion of accord between the two nations – and their two dictator leaders – had been shattered, World War Two took on a decisive phase in the East. The conflict of ideology was reflected in the vast scale of the combat between Nazi Germany and communist USSR. The titanic battles fought between 1941 and the summer of 1943 were on an altogether different level to the fighting elsewhere, no more so than

in the cauldron of Kursk in July 1943.

The town that gave its name to the battle was a relatively small city 280 miles south of Moscow. The actual battle was fought over a 120-mile-wide salient, where the Germans were attempting to pinch out a bulge in their frontline and regain the attacking initiative across the whole theater.

The resultant Operation Citadel led to the largest ever tank battle, the greatest loss of aircraft in a single day, and the commitment of nearly three

million men into some of the most intense fighting in human history. World War Two is littered with pivotal moments, but the outcome of Kursk, perhaps more than any other, determined the outcome of the war. Never again would Hitler be able to go on the concerted offensive, and the long bloody march to Allied victory had gained an unstoppable momentum.

And yet, just as the Russians were engaged in such momentous clashes

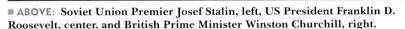
■ ABOVE: Soviet Union Premier Josef Stalin, left, US President Franklin D. Roosevelt, center, and British Prime Minister Winston Churchill, right.

with the Germans, the Allies were embroiled in often bitter argument as to the conduct of the war. The disputes revolving around the clamor for a "second front" now reached new heights.

Ever since the start of the war in the East, Josef Stalin and the Soviet high command had demanded that the British and then the Americans relieve the pressure on the USSR by opening up substantial attacks on German forces in the West. This

pressure for a second front exposed the tensions between supposedly united Allies working toward a single goal.

At the heart of the dispute lay differences over immediate objectives. But it was also about the long-term maneuvering for position in expectation of what the post-war world would be like. It signified the predictable differences between the capitalist USA emerging as the dominant world power, the rise of the communist Soviet Union as a direct opponent, and the decline of Britain and her empire.

Stalin feared the Americans and British would still be prepared to come to terms with Hitler in order to contain communism; Roosevelt and the Americans harbored grave doubts as to Stalin's land grabs with his forces storming westward; the British – and in particular Churchill – were seeking to cling onto their empire via the defense of Suez, North Africa, and the

Mediterranean. The route via Italy also offered the prospect of cutting across the Soviet advance.

Stalin's growing impatience for the second front came to a head in November 1943 when the three leaders met together in Tehran, Iran, to discuss strategy and the post-war future. The Soviet dictator played a cunning and adept hand, reminding Roosevelt and Churchill of their previous promises to launch a western offensive in 1942. After a game of political to and fro, agreement was finally reached: The Americans and British would land troops in the west in the spring of 1944. The countdown to D-Day had begun.

But even amongst the British and US, tensions remained and indeed, in some instances, were heightened. The US had been pressing for an invasion over the shortest possible route – across the English Channel to France – as the only realistic option. General George C. Marshall,

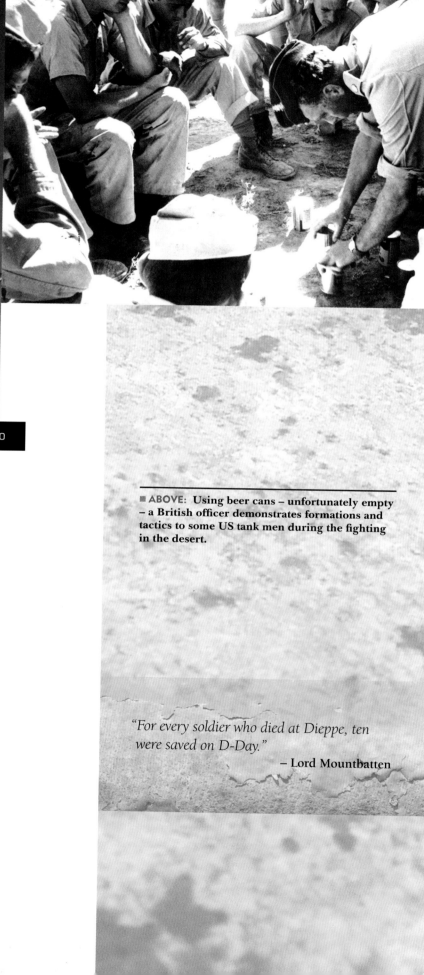

"For every soldier who died at Dieppe, ten were saved on D-Day."

– Lord Mountbatten

the American chief of staff, had long advocated this course. This led to friction with Churchill who preferred to concentrate on the Mediterranean and invasion of Italy as a means to defeat Germany in Europe.

Churchill famously dubbed Italy as the "soft underbelly" of the Axis, citing France as the tough snout of the crocodile that in his imagination represented Hitler's forces. The long and bitter fighting in Italy showed how tough that belly really was, but served to strengthen Marshall's position: France would be the site of the invasion.

In order for it to succeed, the Allies needed to learn from the mistakes of the past, in particular the disastrous Dieppe Raid of August 19, 1942. This test of German defenses around the Channel port was a crushing defeat. The RAF was given a fearful beating, losing 95 aircraft in one day – the highest since the war had begun. Only 10 out of the 24 landing craft that took part in the operation were able to get any tanks ashore. Even those that were landed proved ineffective. Every one of the 27 tanks that reached French soil was destroyed. Of 6,100 men who took part, 4,100 were killed, wounded, or taken prisoner. The Canadians, who made up the bulk of the assault force, in particular suffered appalling casualties – nearly 1,000 were killed.

If there was anything to be gained from their tactical reverse it was the benefit for future actions. As Admiral of the Fleet, Lord Mountbatten, claimed, "For every soldier who died at Dieppe, ten were saved on D-Day." Dieppe showed the planners behind D-Day how an invasion should not be done.

The actual planning for D-Day had begun before the Tehran conference. In August 1943, the Combined Allied Chiefs of Staff met in Quebec and determined that a vast build-up of men and material in England would

be set in motion for an invasion of France.

The chief of staff to the supreme Allied commander drew up the initial plan but the actual commander was not appointed until November 1943. In a sure sign of the balance of power in the American and British relationship, it was General Dwight D. Eisenhower who was given command.

Eisenhower was taking charge of an undertaking that had long been promised but was now becoming reality. Back in the summer when the plans were first being committed to paper – top secret, of course – the project had been given a codename: now Eisenhower, and his staff, officers, and men that he commanded had to put "Operation Overlord" into practice and plan the fighting for real.

■ **LEFT: General George C. Marshall, seated at his desk with a portrait of General Pershing (in background), in the Pentagon building.**

■ **BELOW: British and Canadian prisoners after they had been captured after a failed Allied landing operation in Dieppe, France, August 19, 1942.**

11

Chapter Three:
Overlord

Winter **1943** – June 5 **1944**

■ ABOVE: **"Desert Fox," Rommel, directing operations from his armored vehicle.**

While the Allies formulated their plans, Hitler put Field Marshal Erwin Rommel in charge of improving the Germans' defenses on the French coast. The old "Desert Fox," who had earned the respect of Allied troops for his excellent command of Axis forces in North Africa, would provide a formidable foe for General Eisenhower.

Affectionately known as "Ike," Eisenhower had a style of relative diplomacy and informality that belied the nature of his power within the Allied armed forces. He was made head of Supreme Headquarters Allied Expeditionary Force, or SHAEF. His second-in-command was General Montgomery, who would lead the 21st Army Group. Eisenhower and Monty were often in disagreement over strategy and tactics, but were unified in one immediate goal: they pressed for an increase in troop numbers. The draft plan was revised for an initial assault by five divisions, with a total committal for the campaign of 39 divisions – well over one million men. Not just Americans and British were to take part but also Canadians, Poles, Free French, and other nationalities.

The target would be Normandy. While this went against the accepted wisdom of crossing the Channel at the shortest point, a landing near Calais was fraught with risk. The port there was strongly defended and the terrain away from the shore would be difficult to traverse, with the calamity of the Dieppe Raid weighing heavy in the planners' minds. The beaches of Normandy offered a broader front and better opportunity for success on the first day.

That early progress was vital. For the invasion to succeed, Allied forces would need to gain and hold a beachhead that would enable them to quickly land more troops and supplies. Intelligence had shown that the Normandy area was thinly defended by the Germans. While Hitler's famed "Atlantic Wall" boasted a line of guns, tank traps, barbed wire, mines, and concrete fortifications running from the far north of Norway to the French border with Spain, it was relatively weak in certain places and patchily defended. Normandy, the Allies felt, fitted the bill.

Overlord was, from its inception, a huge enterprise. Men, arms, machinery, and supplies poured into the UK. The war industries of the US and Britain went into overdrive, churning out huge numbers of ships, aircraft, and tanks. It was widely observed that southern England began to resemble one giant army camp, and that the island nation would dip into the sea at its southern coast, so vast was the sheer volume of men, machinery, and heavy weaponry.

The success of Overlord also depended on other, less visible actions: intelligence and surprise were also key elements. While the build-up, training, and tactical planning continued apace, the Allies drew on the skills of code breakers and double agents, a network of spies, and behind-the-line operatives, to monitor the Germans' own

■ BELOW: British and US land and air force leaders – some of the key men behind the total Allied victory in Africa. Left to right are: Air Vice Marshal Broadhurst, AOC Western Desert; Air Marshal Coningham, AOC Tactical Air Force, Mediterranean Theater; General Montgomery, GOC 8th Army; General Alexander, deputy C-in-C under General Eisenhower; Air Chief Marshal Tedder, AOC Inc. Mediterranean; and Brigadier-General L. S. Kuter of the US Army Air Force.

plans and troop movements.

In addition, the plan hinged on one enormous game of bluff – the ingenious and inspired scheme to convince the Nazi high command that the Pas de Calais and Norway were the actual destinations for the Allied invasion force. Operation Bodyguard and its offshoot Operation Fortitude were masterstrokes of deception. Thanks to the work of double agents, the Germans were convinced a complete army group – the 1st US Army Group under the command of General McNair and Lieutenant-General George S. Patton – was poised to invade from the south east of England. Fake army camps, landing craft, and tanks were built to bolster the lie.

It worked almost to perfection. Right up until D-Day itself – even in the first phase of the invasion – Hitler remained convinced the landing would be at Calais, though with typical arrogance, would later claim that he had known all along that Normandy had always been the original target. Not all the Allied planning worked so well, however.

In order to prepare troops for such a major offensive the level of

training was stepped up. While very few men knew of the precise details of the plan, troops on the ground were aware that the launch of the second front was near. Personnel were exposed to live fire exercises to emphasize the danger and seriousness of the task that lay before them.

One exercise in particular proved disastrous, and showed how lethal even preparation could be. At the end of 1943, a special training ground had been set up in and around Slapton Sands in Devon. The nature of the beach and shore was very similar to one of the areas American forces would be landing on for the actual invasion – Utah Beach.

During Exercise Tiger, a live shellfire exercise was used to toughen up troops, many of whom lacked combat experience. It went horribly wrong, however, when confusion over timings resulted in the deaths of soldiers disembarking from their tank landing ships, or LSTs. But there was worse to come. Further out to sea, a convoy of eight LSTs, protected only by a single British corvette, was attacked by a group of nine German

■ **BELOW: British troops training for D-Day at Slapton Sands, Devon.**

14

■ **ABOVE:** Lieutenant-General Patton, America's leading tank expert.

■ **BELOW:** Men of a US tank division line up their M4 Sherman tanks on a range in England to get in a round of firing practice with their 75mm guns; preparations for D-Day reach their climax, May 9, 1944.

E-boats. One LST was sunk, two more were set on fire, while another was hit by Allied munitions.

The two incidents combined cost the lives of 946 American servicemen, including 10 officers who had the top-rated "BIGOT" status that meant they were among the very few commanders who were in possession of the details of Overlord. Had their bodies been recovered by the Germans, the plans could have been revealed and thrown into disarray. Instead, with macabre fortune, the corpses were all retrieved by the Allies.

Communication errors, a lack of lifebelt training, and inadequate protection were to blame at Slapton, and provided a salutary warning of the need for the utmost vigilance and co-ordination for the actual invasion. But it was also a reminder of what many among the Allied command dreaded. Churchill was haunted by the disastrous beach landings at Gallipoli in World War

One, a strategic blunder of his own making when he was First Lord of the Admiralty. The British Prime Minister feared casualty rates of 50% among the first wave of 160,000 troops to land on D-Day; others felt the slaughter would be even higher.

If there were any doubts about Overlord, however, its momentum was unstoppable. The start date was put back to May 31, 1944. Allied aircraft began to drop greater quantities of arms to the French Resistance and to bomb transport infrastructure in the north of France in order to hinder German reinforcements. Midget submarines were sent over the Channel for intrepid specialists to covertly test the suitability of French beaches to withstand heavy Allied armor.

In March, Eisenhower moved his command from central London to Bushy Park in the suburbs. By April, the operation that he headed was now set. The invasion would take place between Le Havre and Cherbourg

and be split into two sectors: British and Canadian forces would land between Merville in the east and Arromanches in the west across three beaches codenamed Gold, Juno, and Sword; further to the west, the Americans would assault Omaha and Utah beaches in readiness for a thrust to cut off the Cotentin Peninsula. On either side of the theater of operations, airborne paratroop operations would secure the flanks.

The objective was to overcome coastal defenses and drive into the Normandy countryside up to a depth of 10 miles, including much of the regional capital of Caen. It was a bold ambition for the first day of fighting. Many Allied officers expected the reality to be somewhat different. But the moment of battle drew ever nearer.

The actual day of D-Day was revised again to take account of suitable tides and moons: June 5 would be the new start date. The last amphibious exercises had taken place. Sealed within the camps along the 10-mile restriction zone of the English south coast, and air and naval bases, the legions of troops, airmen, and sailors waited for their moment of destiny. It took five days to load the ships, such was the size of the invading force. The fear and tension for some – contemplating the prospect of imminent death amid the chaos and frenzy of lethal combat – became unbearable.

And then the weather intervened. On June 2, Eisenhower had moved to Southwick House, near Portsmouth, the HQ of Admiral Sir Bertram Ramsey who was naval commander-in-chief for the invasion. At Southwick, Eisenhower awaited favorable meteorological reports that would enable him to give the order to go. But the weather was poor. A storm was approaching from the west. High winds and rough seas would play havoc with air and naval operations.

■ **ABOVE: US General Lesley J. McNair.**

■ **BELOW: Southwick House, Portsmouth. Eisenhower's headquarters where the final phase of D-Day planning took place.**

On the other side of the Channel, Rommel took the bad weather as a sign the invasion would not take place for a few more days, and returned to Germany for his wife's birthday.

The commanders agreed on June 4 to postpone for another 24 hours. The next day, there was a break in the weather. A window of opportunity had presented itself, but it was a narrow one. Tides would soon count against the invasion and the whole operation would be set back at least two weeks. A decision had to be made. At 4.15 a.m., Eisenhower made the call to launch the invasion. D-Day was now at hand.

Among the thousands of servicemen now about to play their part in the making of history, junior officers opened their sealed orders to find out what their specific task would be. Eisenhower's message emphasized the momentousness of the undertaking:

"Soldiers, Sailors, and Airmen of the Allied Expeditionary Force! You are about to embark upon a great crusade, toward which we have striven these many months. The eyes of the world are upon you... The tide has turned! The free men of the world are marching together to victory!"

Chapter Four:

The Commanders
Eisenhower & Rommel

Dwight D. Eisenhower

As Supreme Commander Allied Expeditionary Forces, Dwight D. Eisenhower had to call on all the skills of strategic planning, negotiation, and authority he had learned and honed in an army career spanning four decades. It says much for his abilities that, despite his absence of combat experience, he was trusted and respected by both his superiors and the troops under his command for his military acumen and the quality of his leadership. Eisenhower was a soldier who could convince, cajole, and inspire other soldiers to lead and to fight.

Dwight David Eisenhower was born in Texas in 1890, but raised in Abilene, Kansas. The third of seven sons, he was born into a Mennonite family that prided itself on its work ethic – the clan from which he sprang called themselves the "Plain People." Encouraged to pursue a military career, Eisenhower looked to join either the Naval Academy at Annapolis or its army counterpart at West Point. He graduated from the latter in 1915.

Knee injuries had curtailed Eisenhower's promising sporting career and, to his own frustration, he missed out on actual combat in World War One. But he excelled at organization and proved a success in early staff assignments, under the command of generals such as Pershing, Krueger, and Douglas MacArthur.

Service in Europe and the Philippines equipped him for the delicate task of working with allies, and by the time Pearl Harbor forced America into World War Two, he had become a brigadier-general. Eisenhower's career was now at a turning point: would he be employed as an adept but deskbound strategist and planner staying behind in the States? Or would he assume command in the places where the actual war was being waged?

Chief of Staff General George C. Marshall had no doubts where Eisenhower's talents would be best

■ **BELOW:** US Lieutenant Dwight D. Eisenhower watches Illinois troops dig trenches during training at San Antonio, Ft. Houston, Texas, in 1916.

employed. He called him first to Washington and then sent him to England to begin the coalition effort to take the war to the Nazis. As Commanding General, European Theater, Eisenhower oversaw the landings in North Africa, Sicily, and Italy. He had proved his mettle; now he was given the ultimate responsibility – to lead the Allied invasion of Western Europe.

This was a hugely testing role. As well as having to plan and organize an operation that required the control of over a million servicemen, Eisenhower had to play a shrewd political game to balance and placate the competing factions under his command. For all their supposed single purpose, the Allies were often at complete loggerheads. Political leaders had their own agendas, exposed in the disagreements between Roosevelt, Churchill, and the Free French leader Charles de Gaulle.

Senior officers vied with each other for power and influence. Mistrust was almost endemic, and generals would brief against other generals. In some cases the resentments boiled over into outright hostility. General Montgomery, for example, was loathed by many, even some of his British compatriots. Yet Eisenhower was able to deal with such tensions and drive the plan forward. It was not an easy course, but Eisenhower proved to be an adept pilot, steering Overlord through some very tricky waters.

The eventual success in Normandy earned Eisenhower promotion to that of General of the Army (5 stars) in December 1944. When the Third Reich collapsed in 1945, Eisenhower was appointed Military Governor, US Occupied Zone, and then took over the newly formed NATO forces in 1951.

His military expertise, negotiating acumen, and affable style made him a natural for political office and he

■ ABOVE: **This is a portrait of the Eisenhower family, made at Abilene, Kansas in 1902. The boys, back row, are, left to right: Dwight, Edgar, Earl, Arthur, and Roy. Between Ike's mother and father, first row, is Milton.**

■ RIGHT: **General Dwight D. Eisenhower, commander-in-chief of Allied operations in North Africa, salutes outside his headquarters on May 8, 1943. In the background are the British and American flags.**

successfully ran for US President in 1952. The qualities of friendliness, optimism, and confidence he had employed as a soldier stood him in good stead during the boom years of the 1950s in which America had emerged as the world's dominant power. "I like Ike" was his peacetime campaign slogan but also a reflection of the esteem he was held in by those who served under him during times of war.

Erwin Rommel

Of all the leading generals of the Wehrmacht, none gained such respect among adversaries, as well as comrades, as Erwin Rommel. While he was not quite the anti-Nazi "good German" as popularly portrayed, there is little doubt as to his brilliance as a battlefield commander.

Born in Heidenheim, in 1891, Rommel joined the German army in 1910. As a lieutenant he fought with great courage on the Western Front and won the Iron Cross. His standing was bolstered by a succession of heroic actions in Italy, culminating in the award of the Pour le Merite honor at the Battle of Caporetto, establishing a reputation for brave and dynamic leadership.

In peacetime Rommel served as a regimental commander and excelled as an instructor and theoretician. By 1935 he had risen to the rank of lieutenant-colonel, and his lectures were published as a book on infantry tactics in 1937. The book was highly influential, and won admiration from Adolf Hitler, who appointed Rommel to his senior command staff.

World War Two provided the arena for Rommel to put his personal experience and his theories into action, and with impressive effect. Rommel was a brilliant exponent of blitzkrieg, leading his 7th Panzer Division on a devastating charge through France. Promoted to general, he was sent to North Africa after the Italians had been routed by the British.

His impact was immediate: the British were driven back to Egypt, threatening Cairo and the Suez Canal and earning Rommel the admiring soubriquet of the Desert Fox from his opponents. But defeat at the hands of the revitalized 8th Army, led by Montgomery, and then attack from the west, by US forces, precipitated Rommel's first major defeat.

■ ABOVE: **Erwin Rommel.**

The admiration of his own troops and enemies however, had been cemented. When news of his appointment as head of the German army in France reached the Allies, they knew full well that they faced a formidable adversary, even if they enjoyed superiority in terms of personnel and material. Rommel was a realist, however, and had pushed for a peace accord between Germany and the Allies in the full knowledge that his nation was heading for defeat.

Yet it was to be the lethal power struggle within the German high command that would be Rommel's ultimate undoing. He was implicated in the plot to assassinate Hitler in 1944. The extent of his involvement, his motivations, and the issue of whether he was a committed Nazi or not, are all subject to continuing debate, but after the plot was foiled, Hitler ensured that Rommel was subject to deadly recriminations.

The Desert Fox, by now a field marshal, had been seriously injured in an Allied strafing attack on July 17, 1944, but his demise would come by his own hand. Faced with the prospect of execution and the persecution of his family for the plot to kill Hitler, he was given the option of an honorable death. He took it and poisoned himself on October 17. Hitler gave him a full state funeral.

21

■ **ABOVE RIGHT: Field Marshal Erwin Rommel, right, Commander of the German Afrika Korps, is shown with Field Marshal Albert Kesselring, German Air Commander, in the Western Desert in Libya, North Africa in September 1942 during World War Two.**

■ **RIGHT: The funeral cortege of Field Marshal Erwin Rommel enroute to Württemberg for burial October 18, 1944.**

Chapter Five:

Pegasus

23.00 hours June 5 – 06.00 hours June 6 **1944**

The aircraft took off from England late on the night of June 5. Just after midnight, the towing cables that had tethered the Horsa gliders to the Halifax bombers, which had brought them across the Channel, were released. The powerless craft were left to their own perilous devices. They swooped through the night air, honing in on their target. Inside the six aircraft were 180 men of the British 6th Airborne Division.

Drawn from a variety of regiments, companies, and platoons, and with a range of specialist skills at their disposal, the young men and officers awaited their fate. A last check of weaponry; a few nervously exchanged songs and jokes to try and still their fear. Then the stern order of silence, with the only sound being the rush of the wind outside the frames of the gliders. The pilots, who had sneaked through a gap between the German flak defenses, now banked their aircraft and prepared to land. The group's objectives were the two key bridges spanning the River Orne and the Caen canal at Benouville and Ranville, between the Normandy city of Caen and the coast. This was to be the site of the first action of the campaign. D-Day had begun.

These airborne landings signaled the first phase of the Allied plan. While American paratroopers from the 82nd and the 101st Divisions prepared to drop over the villages of the Cotentin Peninsula on the western flank, the 6th Airborne were tasked with securing the eastern flank to protect the forthcoming landings on Gold, Juno, and Sword beaches. Three of the gliders headed for the canal bridge. Made out of flimsy plywood, some of them broke up as soon as they landed. The troops of D Company of the Oxford and Buckinghamshire Light Infantry were commanded by Major John Howard. As Howard's craft hit the ground, it

"We heard the glider pilot shout 'Casting off!' and suddenly we were in a silent world. It was like being trapped in a floating coffin in mid-space... the singing, the talk, the conversation stopped. People realised what we were heading for. There was no going back now. We'd reached the point when we could only go forward."

– Private Harry Clark, D Company, 2nd Battalion, Oxford and Buckinghamshire Light Infantry

■ **OPPOSITE:** Troops crossing Pegasus Bridge – a river crossing close to the Normandy beaches invaded on D-Day.

■ **BELOW:** Two of the three gliders at Pegasus Bridge – the cafe and bridge are visible in the rear of the photo.

bounced and skidded and the pilots were knocked senseless. But they had done their job. The glider came to a juddering halt within 20 yards of the target.

Howard and his men spilled out of the glider. A lone German sentry failed to raise the alarm, mistakenly thinking the landing glider was an airplane that had crashed elsewhere. With faces blackened, and armed with sub machine guns, rifles, and grenades, soldiers from D Company went into action immediately. Pillboxes on the western bank of the canal were taken out with grenades. A platoon led by Lieutenant Den "Danny" Brotheridge ran across the bridge to capture the opposite side. Alerted by the grenade explosions, German defenders sprang into action themselves. A deafening fire fight broke out and, in the blaze of noise and combat, Brotheridge was shot and mortally wounded. He was to be the first Allied soldier to be hit as a result of enemy fire on D-Day.

The 6th Airborne had lost other men, Lance-Corporal Fred Greenhalgh, who drowned when

■ **ABOVE: British vehicles crossing a Bailey bridge built over the Caen canal, France.**

his glider landed in a pond, and Wirelessman Everett who was killed when his platoon was dropped off course. As more British troops poured over the bridge, Lieutenant Sandy Smith ignored the arm he had broken on landing and led his men to secure the eastern end. The bridge had been taken, and word soon came through that the other over the River Orne had been captured without a shot being fired. From the other detachment of three gliders, one had landed

eight miles off course near the River Dives, but the soldiers were able to move swiftly through the village of Ranville and avoid contact with the enemy, meeting up on the bridge with platoons from the other gliders.

This early mission had been such a success that it had almost felt like a training exercise rather than combat for real. The element of surprise, in landing gliders under the cover of darkness and near complete silence, had been executed almost to

perfection. Casualties were mercifully light. The troops had been intensely primed and trained physically hard, and their fitness and preparation proved to be key elements in the success of the action.

The capture of the bridges was an early victory, but in order to ensure there would be protection for Montgomery's left flank, reinforcements would be swiftly required to repel the expected counterattack. Subsequent

■ **ABOVE:** Actor Richard Todd reminisces with Major John Howard on a model of the Pegasus Bridge at the newly opened D-Day Museum at the Browning Barrack, Aldershot, England.

position was still precarious. Shortly after the initial landings, troops from the 7th Parachute Battalion arrived to relieve and strengthen the bridgehead. The actor Richard Todd was part of this force; he would later play Howard in the film *The Longest Day*. The presence of Todd's commanding officer provided a darkly comic twist that appealed to the gallows humor of many of the British soldiers: the officer's name was Lieutenant-Colonel Pine-Coffin.

■ **RIGHT: Pegasus Bridge in more recent times.**

paratrooper drops did not go according to plan. The 9th Battalion of the Parachute Regiment were scattered far and wide, severely hindering their assault on the gun battery at Merville in which they incurred heavy casualties. Large amounts of kit and weaponry – including valuable anti-tank guns – were lost.

Back at the two bridges, Howard's men fought off a small-scale assault by two German half tracks, but their

Chapter Six:
The Battle Begins
Midnight June 6 – 10.00 hours June 6 **1944**

■ **BELOW:** American paratroopers passing through the street of St. Mere Eglise, 1944.

While the vast seaborne armada of 5,000 ships were sailing for Normandy, and British paratroops secured the eastern flank, almost 50 miles away their American counterparts had been plunged into fierce fighting at the southern neck of the Cotentin Peninsula. Their objective had been to secure the beach exits at Utah and establish footholds in the hinterland. Sent into action at night behind enemy lines, dropping from C-47 Skytrains (known as Dakotas by the British), or carried by gliders running a gauntlet of enemy flak, the men of the 101st and 82nd Airborne Divisions went into action.

An unexpected bank of fog played havoc with the drops. Aircraft were shot down, groups of paratroopers, or sticks, were scattered over the area, drop zones were missed, equipment lost, and whole battalions broken up. Descending paratroopers were machine-gunned by German soldiers, inflicting further losses to the Divisions' fighting strength. But with a combination of dogged mend-and-make-do reorganization and no little bravery, the men of the 101st and 82nd rallied and went into battle.

Many swiftly dispensed with the "clicker" devices designed to identify friend from foe and resorted to the code words of "Flash" and

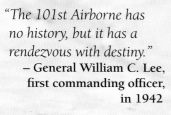

"The 101st Airborne has no history, but it has a rendezvous with destiny."
– General William C. Lee, first commanding officer, in 1942

■ **RIGHT: A statue of Major Dick Winters, unveiled near the beaches where the D-Day invasion of France began in 1944. The bronze statue built near the village of Sainte-Marie-du-Mont, is a tribute to a man whose quiet leadership was chronicled in the book and television series** *Band of Brothers.*

"Thunder." The fighting was bloody, with stories of atrocities on both sides intensifying the kill-or-be-killed brutality. St. Mere Eglise soon became a focal point for the 82nd. A ragtag of units grouped together and took the town amid bitter firefights and close-quarter action.

Closer to the coast, the drops of the "Screaming Eagles" of the 101st had mixed fortunes. Nonetheless, for a division in existence for just two years, its troops performed well and they were able to achieve their objectives in controlling the exits from Utah and gaining important, if tenuous, hold of positions near the Douve river.

German gun batteries were also taken out. It was in one of these engagements later in the day that the men of "Easy" Company, 506 Parachute Infantry Regiment, led by Lieutenant Dick Winters, overcame a force three times their own size and knocked out guns at Brecourt. The exploits of Winters and his men were immortalized in the book and television series, *Band of Brothers.*

Utah was chosen almost as an afterthought but was essential to Overlord. The invasion site of Normandy was selected in part to

■ **ABOVE: US paratroopers fix their static lines before a jump before dawn over Normandy on D-Day June 6, 1944, in France. The decision to launch the airborne attack in darkness instead of waiting for first light was probably one of the few Allied mistakes on June 6, and there was much to criticize both in the training and equipment given to paratroopers and glider-borne troops of the 82nd and 101st Airborne Divisions. Improvements were called for after the invasion; the hard-won knowledge would be used to advantage later.**

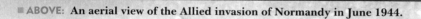

■ ABOVE: An aerial view of the Allied invasion of Normandy in June 1944.

avoid a heavily defended port like Calais or Dieppe. The consequence was that no major port was available to the Allies as they sought to gain an immediate beachhead. Utah, however, offered the lure of Cherbourg 37 miles away.

The seaborne landings here went by and large to plan. At 06.30 hours, following an air bombardment, the initial waves of troops landed successfully. Within minutes almost all the Duplex Drive or DD amphibious tanks were onshore.

Along the eastern end of the invasion, the British and Canadians had contrasting fortunes but met with similar overall accomplishment. The fleet of ships carrying the soldiers of the US 1st Army and the British 2nd Army making their way across the Channel had, mercifully, met little opposition. An air and naval screen had kept the U-boats at bay,

Allied mastery of the air prevented the limited number of Luftwaffe aircraft from attacking the vessels, and minesweepers cleared a safe passage ahead.

Another ingenious ploy used by the Allies was "window," the mass drop of strips of aluminum paper designed to confuse German radar. Window was another successful deployment of deception tactics, fooling the Germans into thinking a massive invasion force was heading toward areas other than the Calvados coasts of Normandy where the real invasion was headed.

As a result the ships steamed purposefully toward their destinations. On board the men readied themselves for battle. Weighed down with kit, nerves jangling, their morale was stiffened by Eisenhower's stirring call to arms read out over Tannoys, and the broadcast

of appropriate music. On board one ship the bagpipe player, Bill Mullin, attached to the 1st Special Service Brigade of Commandos, played traditional Scottish songs.

For those defending the shore in pillboxes and observation positions, when the ships peered into view through the early morning gloom it presented an extraordinary and terrifying sight. While German defenses were patchy and still confused by deception operations – including the drop of fake paratroop dummies – the sheer size of the invasion fleet was unmistakable.

And then the Allied guns opened up. From battleships, cruisers, destroyers, and other vessels, a devastating fusillade of shells and rockets was aimed at the beach defenses. The naval bombardment shook the attackers almost as much as those the munitions were aimed at.

■ **ABOVE:** US army soldiers disembark from a landing craft during the Normandy landings (D-Day) of June 6, 1944. Sherman tanks and White half tracks can be seen drawn up on the beach.

HMS Belfast was part of bombardment Force E attacking the Gold and Juno sectors and one of the first to go into action. Its 6-inch guns opened up at 05.30 on the battery at Ver-sur-Mer. By the campaign's end, the barrels of *Belfast*'s guns had worn out, such was the intensity of the firing.

While the shelling continued, troops boarded their landing craft or began the charge to the shore in LSTs. In rough waters, seasickness turned the close confines of the craft into nightmarish quarters, and further exhausted men already drained by fear. On board one British vessel officers rallied their men with a rendition of *Jerusalem*. Others read passages from Shakespeare.

Yet, in the British sector at least, many of the fears of appalling losses were misplaced. It was by no means an undamaging landing – withering machine gun fire, artillery, mortars,

and small arms raining down on Allied troops would ensure that – but on Gold, Juno, and Sword beaches, significant progress was made.

The first units of 231st and 69th Brigades reached Gold at 07.25 with DD tanks following in. Three beach exits were cleared within an hour, enabling the steady build-up of troop numbers, though with intense fighting to come. The Canadians on Juno landed half an hour later, but hampered by tide and current, and strong German opposition, the movements of 7th and 8th Brigades became congested and the force came under heavy fire. With great bravery, the Canadians were able to capture

Bernières by 09.30.

On the eastern flank at Sword, a multi-national force landed and was soon engaged in heavy fighting before three exits were cleared within the hour. Free French Commandos, suitably inspired by fighting for the liberation of their own soil, took the heavily defended Riva Bella casino, before the Germans regrouped and held up the advance.

The assault of the Gold-Juno-Sword sector was a success, Utah likewise. The remaining beach was Omaha. It is a name that 70 years on, still resonates with the horrors of what D-Day meant for the lives of so many young servicemen.

■ **BELOW:** German prisoners of war are led away by Allied forces from Utah Beach, on June 6, 1944, during landing operations on the Normandy coast, France.

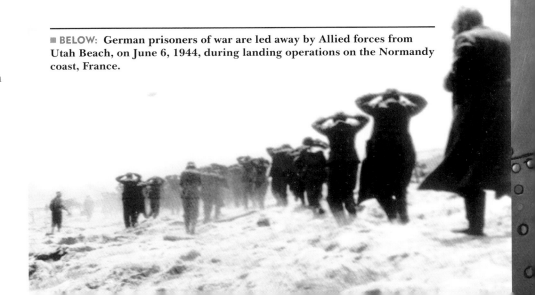

Chapter Seven:
Omaha

05.30 June 6 – 12.00 hours June 6 **1944**

■ **ABOVE:** **Carrying full equipment, American assault troops move onto the beachhead, codenamed Omaha Beach, on the northern coast of France on June 6, 1944.**

The beach that runs westward for five miles between Sainte-Honorine-des-Pertes to Vierville-sur-Mer is a picturesque location dotted with seaside villages and views over the Channel from cliffs and steep escarpments, or bluffs. Today, it is a quiet backwater, but there are still physical reminders of a time when it was the scene of some of the grimmest hours in American military history.

This sector of the landings was codenamed Omaha. It was a vital link between the assaults on Utah and the British-Canadian attacks to the east. It had to be taken to create a unified lodgment across the front and it was, eventually, secured – but at horrific cost.

Omaha presented a different objective to the other beaches. Surrounded by high ground it provided only narrow possible exits and gave an advantageous position to the Germans. Here the defenses were of a more formidable nature. Girders, wooden posts, barbed wire, mines, and tank traps, many of them mined, were embedded along the shoreline. German troops were well dug in in bunkers, pillboxes, artillery emplacements, and machine gun nests, enjoying ideal firing positions.

They were a hard nut to crack, with men drawn from elements of the 352nd Division to supplement those of the main defense force of the 716th Infanterie-Division. While many of

■ **ABOVE:** A US battle monument overlooking Omaha Beach in Normandy, France, which was the inspiration for the Steven Spielberg film *Saving Private Ryan*.

■ **BELOW:** Men of the American assault troops of the 16th Infantry Regiment, injured while storming Omaha Beach during the Allied invasion of Normandy, wait by the chalk cliffs at Colleville-sur-Mer for evacuation to a field hospital for further treatment, June 6, 1944.

the defenders across Normandy were non-German personnel and prisoners drafted in from conquered lands in the east, the Wehrmacht forces at Omaha presented an opposition relatively well-manned, equipped, and secure, and motivated to follow Hitler's demand to throw the invaders back into the sea.

Other factors worked against the initial American wave of combat teams from the 1st and 29th Divisions. The air and naval bombardment was ineffective; rocket volleys fell short and exploded harmlessly in the water; not a single bomb dropped on Omaha landed on the beach, thus failing to destroy any of the defenses, nor making craters for the invading troops in which to take shelter.

Rough seas again hampered operations, but at Omaha, amphibious tanks were launched too far from the shoreline. Setting off at up to 5,000 meters from the beach, 27 of the 32 tanks of the 741st Tank Battalion were sunk by the waves. The lack of armor on the beach was to prove fatal.

Landing craft that were also launched too far out struggled to contend with the waves. Those that did close in were hit by accurate fire. Ten sank. By the time those that had survived the conditions reached the beach, a murderous hail of fire awaited the soldiers. Rounds pinged off the metal structures and as the ramps dropped, troops were cut down before they could even get off the craft.

Men that did survive plunged into the water or stumbled through the surf, weighed down by too much equipment and ammunition. It was a scene of utter carnage. The dead and wounded floated in the water, explosions, smoke, and the ceaseless buzz of bullets wreaked devastation on the surviving Americans, desperately seeking any kind of protection and rendered unarmed

with weaponry jammed by sand and saltwater. Many men were paralyzed with fear; some, driven crazy by the fighting, walked around in a daze or screamed like men possessed. The disastrous nature of the landing broke up whole companies and, with a lack of protective armor, the attack had descended into a terrifying, chaotic nightmare.

The situation was so serious that at one stage commanders considered a withdrawal and to send subsequent waves to Utah. But with the arrival of some tanks, the reorganization

■ **ABOVE: The view overlooking Utah Beach from Pointe du Hoc, in Normandy, France.**

■ **BELOW: This is the scene along a section of Omaha Beach in June 1944, during Operation Overlord. Landing crafts put troops and supplies on shore at Omaha, one of five landing beaches. Seen in the background is part of the large fleet that brought the Allied troops across the English Channel. Barrage balloons are flying in the air, designed to entangle low-flying enemy aircraft in their cables.**

instilled by senior officers, and unbelievable bravery from men of all ranks, the Americans rallied. It was at around 08.00 that Colonel George Taylor, commander of the 1st Division's 16th Infantry Regiment, issued his famous call to arms. "The only people on this beach are the dead and those that are going to die – now let's get the hell out of here!"

By this time, after a tortuous journey to reach their destination, the 2nd Rangers Battalion had begun its climb up the cliff to the west to take the gun battery at Pointe du

"Every man who set foot on Omaha Beach that day was a hero."
– General Omar Bradley

■ **ABOVE:** The hulks of wrecked landing craft and sunken vessels, which formed a breakwater for ships in the D-Day landing at Omaha, are shown in this photograph a year after the historic events.

Hoc. Showing immense courage, the men of the Rangers scaled the sheer face under fire using grappling hooks and ladders, only to find the bunkers empty, with the guns that were their target sited away from the cliff edge. These were captured, but the 2nd would fight a desperate battle to hold on to their position under frequent attack from the 916th Grenadier Regiment for another 24 hours yet.

Down on the beach, other units were able to move forward under relatively less severe fire. The 5th Ranger Battalion landed (they had originally been set to join the attack on Pointe du Hoc) and with assistance from some tanks and crucial close-quarters fire from destroyers, which had sailed near to the sector, the Americans began to make some kind of progress. The fighting would be intense and costly, the situation on the beach a day-long scene from hell, but at last troops were able to get off the sand and shingle, move up the bluffs, and fire back at the enemy that had ended the lives of so many compatriots. By midday, Omaha was still one unholy mess but the village of Vierville was captured and the momentum began to swing the Americans' way.

Omaha now is a place of pilgrimage for Americans who visit the museums and cemeteries that commemorate their nation's fallen. US casualty estimates for D-Day at Omaha range between 2,000 and 3,000. The precise figure is still unclear, but what is certain is that the assault was one of the gravest ever inflicted on American arms. As General Bradley said, "I have returned many times to honor the valiant men who died on that beach. They should never be forgotten. Nor should those who lived to carry the day by the slimmest of margins. Every man who set foot on Omaha Beach that day was a hero."

33

■ **BELOW:** In this aerial view, in a symbolic gesture to strengthen ties and understanding between France and the United States, 3,000 people join to form the phrase "France will never forget" on the once-bloody sands of the D-Day landing site, Omaha Beach.

Chapter Eight:
The Long Day Closes

June 6 – June 9 **1944**

■ **BELOW:** Air reconnaissance photographs of the Normandy coast, between Cherbourg and Le Havre. Defensive flooding near Carentan, about 7 miles inland on the Cherbourg-Caen railway in June 1944, photographed from the air before the Allied landings began on June 6. The town of Carentan itself was occupied by advancing Allied troops on June 12, 1944.

While the Americans were precariously pinned down on the beach at Omaha, the Allies were making steady, if unspectacular, progress elsewhere. At Utah, by mid-morning six battalions from the US 4th Infantry Division had followed the initial wave and three beach exits had been secured. With six battalions now onshore, the capture of the La Madeleine defensive position further strengthened the foothold.

Pouppeville was liberated at midday, and with troops infiltrating

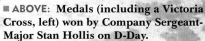

■ **ABOVE: Medals (including a Victoria Cross, left) won by Company Sergeant-Major Stan Hollis on D-Day.**

"Eventually the pillbox was silenced. That was when I saw my first dead Germans. Gruesome. I thought those chaps had probably been called up for service like myself and had no wish to be where they were. They didn't stand a chance, really."
– **Lance Corporal Norman Travett, 2nd Battalion, Devonshire Regiment**

further inland, the invasion forces were able to link up with the airborne troops of the 101st who had dropped the night before. By the end of D-Day, over 23,000 servicemen had been landed with around 200 casualties. By comparison, the US airborne divisions had incurred losses 10 times that number.

In the British sector to the east, there was similar success, albeit against tougher resistance. At Gold, there was an intense battle at Le Hamel, where the 1st Battalion of the Royal Hampshires were given a severe test. They were only able to take the town with the aid of the 2nd Devonshires in the late afternoon.

■ **ABOVE:** Royal Marine commandos moving off the Normandy beaches during the advance inland from Sword beach.

Commandos set off for Port-en-Bessin to try and link up with the Americans, helping to relieve the pressure at Omaha.

As ever, there were many tales of collective and individual heroism, but at Gold the actions of Company Sergeant-Major Stan Hollis, of the 6th Battalion Green Howards, stood out. As described in the official citation the 31-year-old "went with his company commander to investigate two German pillboxes which had been by-passed as the company moved inland. Hollis instantly rushed straight at the pillbox, firing his Sten gun. He jumped on top of the pillbox, re-charged his magazine, threw a grenade in through the door and fired into it, killing two Germans and taking the remainder prisoners."

Later that day Hollis took out a field gun with a PIAT (a hand-held anti-tank weapon) from a house at 50 yards range. On discovering that two of his men were still in the house, he drew enemy fire and the two men were able to escape. For such actions, Hollis was awarded the highest British medal for gallantry, the Victoria Cross, the only to be awarded that day.

Further inland at Brazenville came one of the decisive engagements of D-Day. Oberstleutnant Meyer's *Kampfgruppe* of three battalions from the 352nd Division had been sent on a chase to Carentan to attack Allied invasion "forces" – the exploding

dummies that played a part in the deception operation. Ordered to turn and counter the threat at Gold, and already damaged by Allied fighters, Meyer's group was utterly defeated by the British 69th Brigade, which inflicted a huge casualty rate. Less than 100 of the *gruppe*'s force of 3,000 men were able to return to their division, while Meyer himself was killed in the fighting.

By 16.00 hours, the British had moved on to Arromanches and by nightfall, elements of the 50th Division were on the outskirts of Bayeux. After a day in which 25,000 men had been brought ashore for the loss of around 1,000 casualties, there was enormous symbolism in the advance to the town that gave its name to the tapestry depiction of another cross-Channel invasion almost 900 years before.

Having established a bridgehead of six miles along the coast and inland, the British were able to link up with units at Juno. Here the Canadians battled bravely to overcome considerable opposition (perhaps second only in intensity to that at Omaha), suffering over 900 casualties.

Several beach exits had been cleared by mid-morning, and despite overcrowding on the beach, advances were made to Banville, St. Croix, and Langrune. By 14.00, the whole of the Canadian 3rd Division, under the command of Major-General

■ **ABOVE:** Britain's King George VI visited a Normandy beachhead on June 16, and drove toward the battle scene. At General Montgomery's advanced HQ, he conferred a number of decorations on members of the Allied forces. His Majesty presents the CBE to Major-General Rod Keller, of the Canadian 3rd Division, for distinguished service with the Canadian Army.

Rod Keller, was on land and further advanced than any other Allied force. A push inland to a depth of seven miles held out the tantalizing promise of capturing the airfield at Carpiquet, but a lack of ammunition and fear of a concerted counterattack resulted in a frustrating halt.

There was stiff resistance too at Sword and, with the tide rapidly coming in, a worrying build-up on the beach ensued until German emplacements were overrun by noon. Infiltration inland was difficult, as thousands of troops and armor congested the narrow lanes. Lovat's Commandos were able to reach the 6th Airborne Pegasus Bridge, but a counterattack by the 21st Panzer Division, though only partial and lacking momentum, at Periers Ridge, halted a more concerted Allied advance.

Elsewhere, the British stalled. A particularly long and vicious battle was fought for the Hillman strongpoint, while a lack of mechanized armor, and co-ordination problems between infantry and tank units, meant the 185th Brigade could not reach the planned objective of Caen. Instead the city was heavily

bombed, with damaging ramifications for the later campaign.

While the British had advanced six miles with the landing of nearly 30,000 troops and the cost of 1,000 casualties, success was mixed. But what would the brave, embattled, shattered troops at Omaha have given for such progress? Nearly 35,000 men were crammed into a tiny beachhead measuring five miles by little over one-mile deep. Three men had won the Congressional Medal of Honor but at a terrible cost.

The overall situation at the end of D-Day was not the overambitious success Montgomery had envisaged but neither was it the disaster others had feared. Land forces had taken on their overstretched German counterparts and proved strong enough to prevail, by and large. Had the Luftwaffe been able to mount attacks from the air, it might have been a different story, but such was the RAF and USAAF's domination of the skies that the threat was almost totally negated. While exact casualty figures are difficult to ascertain, it is thought the Allies lost 10,000 soldiers, sailors, airmen, and glider pilots, with 2,500 killed, though

some estimates suggest nearly 5,000 died on the day. German losses were in the region of up to 9,000.

The Allies now seized the opportunity to exploit their foothold and pour in reinforcements and supplies. Key to this phase of the campaign were the Mulberry harbors. Without a substantial port facility to call on along the Calvados coast, the Allies instead utilized an ingenious and ambitious idea to construct artificial breakwaters, piers, and roadways. Many senior officers scoffed at the idea but, once the huge concrete caissons were built around Britain and then towed slowly into place, they proved to be superbly effective.

Two harbors began to be assembled just three days after D-Day: one at Omaha, the other at Arromanches. A storm on June 19 wrecked the former but the latter, swiftly named Port Winston, lasted another eight months, bringing ashore 2.5 million men, 500,000 vehicles, and 4 million tons of supplies.

All those men and all that material would be invaluable. D-Day may have ended but the battle for France was only just beginning.

■ **BELOW:** **For the first time in history, an invading army has taken its own harbor to the enemy-held shore. The colossal task of planning and constructing a prefabricated, floating harbor big enough to supply the Allied armies in France was carried out in the period between the 1943 Quebec conference and D-Day in June 1944. Huge concrete caissons, each weighing 7,000 tons, were towed across the 100 miles of Channel and set down at Arromanches on the Normandy coast, where 15 obsolete ships had been sunk to form a preliminary harbor arm. Floating piers and pier heads were all made in sections and towed across the sea. In spite of a storm of winter strength, the harbor was completed.**

Chapter Nine:

Tanks versus 88mm

With D-Day now over, the Allies were set to implement phase two and battle through Normandy and beyond. As well as air power and troops on the ground, they would require huge amounts of armor if they were to defeat the Germans' Army Group B and have any hope of success. The clash of armor was pivotal to the campaign – and the contest between Allied tanks and German artillery was key.

Sherman Tank

The principal tank used by US forces throughout the war, the M4 "Sherman," was the mainstay of Allied mechanized armor during the Normandy campaign. It was named after American Civil War commander William Tecumseh Sherman.

The Sherman was a good all-rounder. What it lacked in firepower, strength, and armor it countered with its reliability, cost effectiveness, speed, and mobility. A total of 49,324 Sherman tanks were manufactured between 1942 and 1946, illustrating its mass-produced, workhorse nature.

Shermans had a crew of five – a commander, gunner, loader, driver, and co-driver/hull gunner – and weighed about 33 tons, all powered by a 425-500 horsepower engine. By the time Operation Overlord was underway, the model had been fitted with an upgraded 76mm high-velocity gun.

This jack-of-all-trades' use, however, led to problems on the battlefield. The Sherman was neither an out-and-out infantry support tank nor a heavy battle tank. While numerically superior, Shermans could not compete equally with the Germans' medium Panzer V and especially the heavy Pz. VI "Tiger" in tank-v-tank engagements, with devastating consequences for some actions during the Normandy campaign.

Alongside the M4, the Allies drew on the Cromwell and Crusader tanks,

■ **BELOW: A Luftwaffe airman keeps watch using binoculars beside an anti-aircraft (flak) gun at Essentucki Airfield in the Caucasus region of the Soviet Union.**

which were even less effective in taking on German armor. What the Allies could pit against the Panthers and Tigers was the Firefly. A British adaptation of the Sherman, it was fitted with the British 17-pounder gun, that offered much-improved firepower. While the British waited for their new generation of tanks to come into production with the 17-pounder, Shermans were modified to carry the new armament. Montgomery's 21st Army Group had 342 Fireflies for the D-Day landings, with more coming into action as the battle progressed.

As a result, many British tank troops were composed of three regular Shermans and one Firefly. The Allies now had a mechanized weapon to reckon with. Sheer numbers also counted; a single British armored division could field 700 tanks, as many of the Panzer V and Tiger VI in the whole of the German army in the West put together. But these tanks of the Third Reich were still much feared by the Allies, in no small part due to their armament: the legendary 88mm gun.

The Flugabwehr-Kanone 8.8cm (88mm Flak gun)

Of all the German weaponry of World War Two, the 88mm Flak gun arguably ranks as the best. Designed for use as an anti-aircraft piece, its versatility meant it was used as an anti-tank weapon, an artillery gun, and an anti-infantry weapon. It was reliable, offered a rapid rate of fire, and was deadly accurate across a range of distances. It excelled in almost every discipline. Small wonder that an unnamed Australian soldier once quipped blackly that it was "anti bloody everything."

The 88mm had such a reputation that even the suspicion that it was deployed on the battlefield could have

a dispiriting impact on opposition forces. It was held responsible for more damage than it actually deserved; Allied troops often believed it had destroyed targets when other armaments or weaponry were actually responsible.

88s could easily pierce through Allied tank armor and were highly effective in protecting the Normandy beaches until they were knocked out by Allied forces. When paired with German tanks, the 88mm gained another even more frightening aura. Pz. VI Tiger Is were expensive to make, limited in their movement, and had such high fuel consumption that they were limited in their effectiveness, but with an 88mm gun at their disposal, they could be devastatingly destructive and would often cause panic among Allied tank crews and infantry. This was to be a feature of the vicious fighting to come in France during the summer of 1944.

■ **ABOVE: A Sherman US-built 30-ton tank, in action. The General Shermans were heavily armed and armored, and had a speed of 30 mph.**

"The 88mm is anti bloody everything."
– **Anonymous Australian soldier**

Chapter Ten:
Villers-Bocage
and the Cotentin Peninsula

June 10 – June 26 **1944**

Even as Allied units fought to link up the various beachheads into one unified front, and the first components of Mulberry were towed into place, Adolf Hitler and his sycophants in the German high command remained convinced that the real invasion would still take place elsewhere. "The main thrust must be expected at any moment in the Pas de Calais," ran a communiqué to General Jodl.

It was a pitiful error of intelligence. The 59 German divisions in the West in June 1944, such as the Panzer Lehr, Hitler Jugend, and a number of SS divisions, may have been far from full strength, but they would still impose heavy losses upon the Allies. To compound their disadvantage in terms of numbers of men and weaponry, however, the inertia in deploying them where they could be most effective was critical.

Allied mastery of the skies was also crucial. Before the invasion, bombers and attack aircraft had destroyed key transport connections in the rear to hamper German troop movement and resupply. Now the airmen of the USAAF and RAF constantly attacked units closer to the front, to Rommel's despair.

Nonetheless, the Desert Fox was still able to inflict punishing reverses on Allied positions. One aspect in his favor was that much of the terrain of this part of Normandy was "bocage" country. This was traditional farmland characterized by high hedges and

■ ABOVE: **Germany's General Alfred Jodl.**

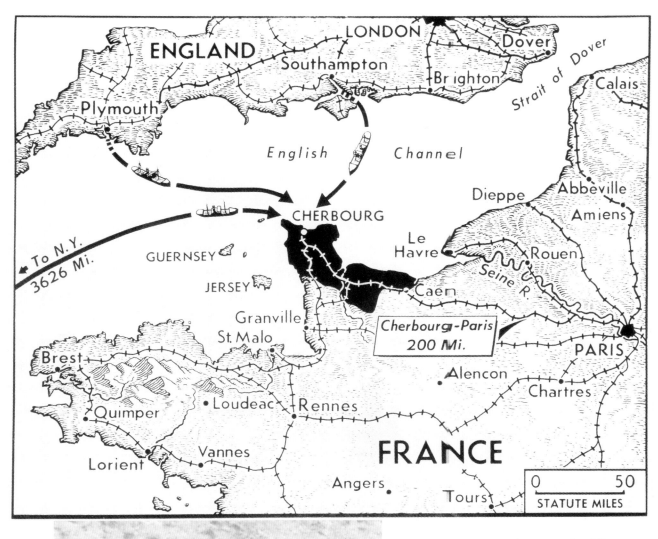

ABOVE: A map showing the D-Day invasion targets.

deep sunken lanes between small fields. It provided ideal defensive positions and a tortuous environment for attacks.

In the west, the Americans tried to break out across the Cotentin Peninsula with the aim of cutting off German forces and capturing the port of Cherbourg. The bocage rendered movement for the US VII Corps difficult. Progress was initially slow, casualties high, and men's nerves were shredded by the lack of visibility and the constant threat of deadly

surprise around the next corner, or over the next hedgerow. By June 18, however, the 9th Division had reached Barneville on the western coast of the peninsula and the push north progressed in earnest. The garrison at Cherbourg finally surrendered on June 26, but after having rendered much of the already damaged port unusable.

The British and Canadians found the going even more treacherous. Caen, the supposed D-Day objective, seemed a long way away now. German

counterattacks meant the Allies suffered brutal localized reverses amid claims of atrocities on both sides, with the SS units in particular involved. As the Germans were unable to press home any advantage and the Allies were restricted for movement as more and more troops poured into the squeezed front, the situation bogged down in a grim and vicious stalemate.

The 7th Armoured Division also found the going tough. The Division had made their name in North Africa as the Desert Rats, but the claustrophobic terrain of Normandy was far different from the open desert plains of Egypt and Libya. In order to try and break the impasse around Caen, the 7th Armoured, under Major-General Erskine, was ordered to switch to the west, outflank the Panzer Lehr and launch a "right hook" to target the strategically vital

town of Villers-Bocage.

Brigadier Robert Hinde's 22nd Armoured Brigade would lead the attack, starting on June 12. Hinde's nickname was "Looney," which in the crazed circumstances of how the battle turned out would have a sickly twist. The operation began well as tanks slipped through a gap in the line opened up by American units and swiftly advanced. By the early morning of June 13, a combined tank and infantry force of the 4th County of London Yeomanry – the "Sharpshooters" – and a company from the 1st Battalion Rifle Brigade were in Villers-Bocage, receiving a gleeful welcome from liberated inhabitants.

The joy was short lived, however. With rumors rife of German 88mm guns trained on the British, the lead units headed out of the town to gain position on the high ground of Point 213. They were stunned by a group of Tiger tanks and a Mark IV Special of the 101st SS Heavy Panzer Battalion. Under the command of a young tank ace called Obersturmführer (captain) Michael Wittmann, the

■ ABOVE: The British advance south of Le Beny Bocage, through wooded and hilly country, continues. This is very difficult country for tanks and they mostly keep to the roads and tracks. Bren carriers move cautiously along a lane south of Le Beny Bocage on June 8, 1944. The German positions are in the high ground in the distance.

Germans simply devastated the Sharpshooters' and Rifle Brigade's lead elements. Within 10 murderous minutes, Wittmann led an attack that destroyed around 20 Cromwell tanks, four Fireflies, and numerous other vehicles, not to mention inflicting around 200 casualties.

Wittmann later returned to wreak similar devastation again in the town

but was eventually – and bravely – repelled. Hinde's men held on to the town but with the 7th Armoured vulnerable to further attacks, the order to withdraw was given on June 14. Villers-Bocage was subsequently bombed in two heavy Allied air raids and was finally liberated for good on August 4.

The setback at Villers-Bocage prevented the hoped-for breakout around Caen. Montgomery's grand plan had floundered, and at considerable cost. However, the battles here had at least meant that the Germans had concentrated much of their forces on the British sector, fearing a breakthrough at Caen and then rapid expansion to the south and east.

This stretched German forces in the west, providing an opportunity for the Americans to launch their own breakout. This had not been the original intention of Montgomery, but for the overall progress of the campaign, there was at least some compensation for the losses around Caen. With the Cotentin Peninsula in US hands, the big push neared.

■ **ABOVE:** An aerial view looking toward Barneville in France on June 26, 1944, shows smoke at the point of battle between advancing Allied forces and Germans.

■ **BELOW:** Villers-Bocage, Normandy town of shattered houses and bomb-cratered streets, is in Allied hands. The Germans had made the town into a strong point in their defensive system, and the Royal Air Force were called in to soften the position.

Chapter Eleven:
The Battle for Caen

July 4 – July 20 **1944**

■ **ABOVE: Although Canadian troops occupied the village of Carpiquet on July 4, it was some days before they managed to gain final possession of Carpiquet Airfield. The airfield, which was built by the British and French at the beginning of the war, was found to have sustained serious damage when it was finally occupied.**

Previous attempts to break the virtual impasse around Caen had proved costly for both the Allies and the Germans. The Allies' Operation Epsom and Wehrmacht counterattacks had seen horrific combat and undoubted bravery on the part of troops. The Allied VIII Corps lost over 4,000 men in just five days, with over half of that total from the 15th Scottish Division. Two SS Divisions were decimated by artillery and naval fire, combined with assaults from troops and tanks on the bitterly contested frontline.

The fighting descended into a murderous tit-for-tat: the command of "take no prisoners" became increasingly common.

But for all the intensity of the fighting, the breakthrough did not materialize. There were tensions between Eisenhower and Montgomery, with American senior officers angered by "Monty's" apparent caution. While these disagreements and enmities festered, and the build-up was hampered by bad weather that hindered supply, another offensive began to finally seize Caen.

On July 4, almost at the same time as German staff officers were telling Hitler that they still expected the main Allied assault in the West to come in a different area, the Canadian 8th Infantry Brigade attempted to seize Carpiquet Airfield to the west

of the city. Carnage ensued: the Canadians fought a sickening fight to the death against SS units in some of the most vicious combat of the whole campaign.

Carpiquet was at last in Allied hands, but the attack faltered elsewhere. Montgomery finally decided on a frontal attack on the city, preceded by massive RAF raids. On the evening of July 7, 2,500 tons of bombs were dropped on Caen. Most of the population had fled days before but well over 300 civilians were killed.

The bombing did not even have the desired effect. The resulting rubble provided perfect defensive positions while the German forward positions were left relatively undamaged. As a consequence, the Allies suffered heavy casualties as troops and armor moved into the broken city. German troops, many of them SS, resisted with lethal fanaticism. The Germans eventually pulled back but, as British troops stumbled into the ancient center through streets choked with rubble, they were only able to secure the northern half.

Elsewhere on the front, as at the highpoint of Hill 112, the attritional effect of attack and counterattack bled whole divisions dry. Allied casualties rose, including increasing numbers of men suffering from "battle-shock" in the claustrophobic confines of such a congested and bloody arena. The Allies' need to get moving became imperative and Operation Goodwood was launched in an attempt to capture the whole of Caen and the surrounding high flat ground that was better suited to mechanized armor.

Lieutenant-General Sir Miles Dempsey, commander of the British 2nd Army, led the planning. The operation drew on three armored divisions and up to eight tank or armored brigades, and called for a concerted punch through to the Caen-Falaise Plain, with support from the air, plus field and naval artillery.

On the early morning of July 18, the two-and-a-half-hour air assault began, severely damaging but not devastating the German lines, particularly on the vital high ground of the Bourguébus Ridge that gave the Germans excellent lines of fire down toward Caen and the advancing Allied tanks and following infantry.

Coupled with bad weather and a lack of concerted force and co-ordination in the attack, as a consequence the three-day advance petered out and came at inevitable cost. The fighting in the remainder of Caen incurred pitiful numbers of killed and wounded among the infantry. However, not all the losses of up to 400 tanks (many were repairable) were accompanied by the deaths of tank crews. The frontline shifted up to seven miles further

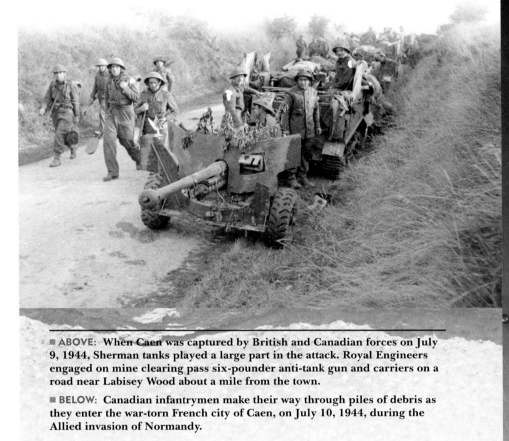

■ **ABOVE:** When Caen was captured by British and Canadian forces on July 9, 1944, Sherman tanks played a large part in the attack. Royal Engineers engaged on mine clearing pass six-pounder anti-tank gun and carriers on a road near Labisey Wood about a mile from the town.

■ **BELOW:** Canadian infantrymen make their way through piles of debris as they enter the war-torn French city of Caen, on July 10, 1944, during the Allied invasion of Normandy.

south and east, and while Goodwood was not the dash to the open country envisaged, caused furious rows within Allied command, and may even have been a localized defeat, it had a strategic benefit. Intended or not the actions of the British and Canadians in the east committed six German divisions to the fighting, further weakening their position in the west to barely more than one effective Panzer division

While the British army was engaged in what has been described as its biggest tank battle, the Americans had taken the town of Saint-Lo after a ferocious and often savage fight across the western sector at the cost of 40,000 American casualties in little more than two weeks. Brigadier-General Norman Cota, one of the heroes of Omaha, was injured in the final assault and entered another Normandy town devastated by weeks of bombing and artillery. Saint-Lo's capture, however, cleared the path for the long-awaited

breakout. And as the fighting briefly abated, the attempt on Hitler's life threw an already confused German command into further recrimination and chaos.

Chapter Twelve:
"Hobart's Funnies"

"The decisive factor on D-Day."
– Sir Basil Liddell-Hart on Hobart
and the 79th Armoured Division

■ **BELOW: British infantry seated on Churchill tanks pass through Le Tourneur on June 8, 1944.**

The Churchill tanks that had been so impotent in the Dieppe Raid found a new lease of life in 1944. For all their faults, the sturdy hulls of the Churchills made them ideal as armored vehicles that could be adapted for specialized use – and their presence in Normandy was vitally important to Allied success.

These tanks became known as "Hobart's Funnies," named after the commander of the 79th Armoured Division to which the tanks were assigned. Major-General Sir Percy Hobart was an experienced and brilliant trainer of tank forces, but had been sidelined to a junior NCO position with the Home Guard until he was restored to active service, playing a key role in North Africa leading the crack 11th Armoured Division. He was

■ ABOVE: **The Churchill Crocodile was the most powerful flame-thrower in the world. This weapon had been constructed to burn out the strong points of the Atlantic Wall and Hitler's fortress. These tanks were used in Normandy.**

regiments were integrated into the various forces landing on D-Day, and in the fighting through Normandy. Among the ingenious tanks of the 79th were:

The Assault Vehicle, Royal Engineers or "AVRE." This adapted Churchill had its main gun replaced with a huge 290mm "Petard Mortar" that fired a 40-pound high-explosive projectile nicknamed the "flying dustbin." It was brutally effective and destroyed a number of otherwise impregnable pillboxes and bunkers.

The **AVRE** could also carry "bobbins" to lay out matting on soft sand, thus providing a surface for heavy armor to cross beaches, and "fascines" – bundles of wood used to traverse ditches and water obstacles.

ARK or **Armoured Ramp Carrier** – a tank fitted with ramps that enabled other vehicles to drive up and over the ARK and avoid obstacles.

Crab – a modified Sherman equipped with a flail that rotated a series of chains to explode mines.

Armored bulldozer – a tank that proved essential in the battle of the bocage for clearing hedgerows.

Crocodiles – Churchill tanks fitted with a flame-thrower that could fire a stream of an early form of napalm over 120 yards.

Duplex Drive or DD tanks – amphibious tanks had been tested as early as 1918, but by 1943 Shermans and Valentines were being developed with canvas flotation screens and propellers as a key component of the seaborne landing of D-Day.

US forces opted not to use the "Funnies" on D-Day but did employ a number of DD tanks, though with mixed success: they were vulnerable if launched away from the shore and in choppy waters, and many sank, taking their crews with them. It has been argued that had the Americans landed some of the other Hobart variants, casualties at Omaha may not have been so severe.

then transferred to set up and train the new 79th Armoured Division.

Hobart's brother-in-law, General Montgomery, recognized the need for specialized vehicles in the Normandy campaign and championed their cause, against considerable opposition – and even contempt – within Allied command. Though Hobart himself did not design the adapted tanks, his advocacy for their use in the 79th Armoured Division was crucial.

The 79th Division did not take part as a single unit but its brigades and

Chapter Thirteen:
Breakout and Counterattack
July 24 – August 7 **1944**

With the frontline reconfigured, both sides in the conflict knew a big push was imminent. The Allies were now more firmly established in Normandy and troops, arms, and supplies were flowing in.

The fighting had been hard, miserable, and bitter, exacting a draining toll on men and morale. But the Germans were being worn down in all sectors in Normandy and did not have the means to significantly reinforce. Within German high command there was a combination of desperation and acceptance that defeat was imminent, countered on the part of some officers with a refusal to accept the reality of the situation, and compounded by Hitler's increasing delusion. His best general, Rommel, was removed from the conflict. Just when unity was required to stem the Allied advance, the botched assassination attempt on the Führer had created a frenzied mix of vicious purges, fear, and paranoia.

In the East the Soviets were storming through in the march to Berlin and had taken 150,000 prisoners in Byelorussia, while the Americans were sending the Japanese into headlong retreat in the Pacific. World War Two was progressing decisively against the Axis powers.

Senior officers within the Wehrmacht hoped to sue for peace with the Western democracies in the hope they could then focus on

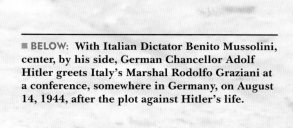

■ **BELOW:** With Italian Dictator Benito Mussolini, center, by his side, German Chancellor Adolf Hitler greets Italy's Marshal Rodolfo Graziani at a conference, somewhere in Germany, on August 14, 1944, after the plot against Hitler's life.

a single front against the USSR. But the Allies had long been in no mood for an accord. The opportunity for US forces to advance in the West of Normandy and south into Brittany would be taken with relish.

General George S. Patton had arrived in France itching to enter the fray. As the deception plans of the 1st Army Group were still active, he was in Normandy in secret. His subordinate, General Lesley McNair, was at the frontline on July 25 at the start of Operation Cobra, observing a massive US air attack on German positions. Some of the bombs dropped short and McNair, along with 111 other US soldiers, was killed by friendly fire. Patton called it "a sad ending and a useless sacrifice," though the raid signaled the start of action that would, at last, let Patton loose on the Germans.

General Bradley's officers had assured journalists that the attack that started on July 25 was not another piecemeal action but the long-promised breakout. The bombing had wrecked already overstretched German forward units. Torn between keeping his divisions against the British and Canadians in the east or switching them to the west, Field Marshal von Kluge, the recently installed commander of Army Group B, could not effectively respond.

Progress for the US VII and VIII corps through the bomb-cratered frontline was initially slow but as German resistance was worn down, a gap opened up and the Americans seized it. General Collins' decision to throw his armored columns in early was bold but productive. Suddenly the impetus changed. Cobra paired tanks and infantry effectively and by the evening of July 26, the pace of advance quickened. German forces were either in un-coordinated retreat or too battered and numbed to resist effectively. US troops observed that their enemy, running out of tanks, ammunition, and personnel, at last had the air of beaten men.

Bradley pounced on the opportunity and called for unremitting attack. On July 27 Coutances was captured. The race to the south continued unabated the next day. It was not a total German collapse – SS units in particular still accounted for fighting of a particularly brutal nature. But with Sherman tanks roaring through open country, this, at last, was the rapid advance the Allies had dreamed of when Overlord was still in its planning stage. In one engagement near St. Denis, a combination of artillery, tank, mortar, and infantry devastated a German column, destroying 96 vehicles and killing 1,150 men.

American spearheads reached and took Avranches on the coast virtually unopposed on July 30. The next day the vital road hub of Pontaubault to the south east was in US hands. Now the route to the south, west, and east lay open. On August 1, Bradley gave Patton the green light to enter the war once more and the 3rd Army was operational.

To the east, where the American sector bordered the British, Operation Bluecoat was launched. This too featured bombing raids preceding an armored advance. Getting tanks and infantry to work in tandem had improved within British forces, so in contrast to Goodwood, the gains made were consolidated more swiftly. A split in the Wehrmacht defenses between the 326th Infanterie Division and the 3rd Paratroop Division enabled tanks from the British 11th Armoured Division to speed five miles behind the German line.

While the XXX Corp and 7th Armoured Division were held up near Villers-Bocage (leading to the sacking of Lieutenant-General Bucknall, Major-General Erskine, and Brigadier "Looney" Hinde),

■ **ABOVE: American infantrymen march past a shattered road block, near Avranches, France on August 4, 1944, as they continue their pursuit of the retreating Germans.**

■ BELOW: **American soldiers start through a hole in thick hedge near Mortain, France, as they advance toward the German positions.**

momentum was with the Allies and, by August 6, after hard fighting, Vire was captured, along with the crucial Mount Pincon.

The Germans' situation was now critical. With the US 4th Armored Division approaching as far south as Rennes, the risk of encirclement of what was left of Army Group B was explicit. Both the Allies and the Nazis knew it. The Germans had either the option to try and escape behind the River Seine – the choice many of the soldiers on the ground desperately hoped for – or one last desperate counterattack. Unsurprisingly, Hitler ordered the latter.

The Führer called for a thrust by the 7th Army between Avranches and Mortain in order to cut across the Americans and isolate the forces in Brittany. Von Kluge was mortified. He knew that this all-or-nothing assault could lead to total defeat, but he was all but powerless to resist. And so, on the night of August 6-7, the German counterattack began.

Without an initial artillery bombardment, the Germans enjoyed an element of surprise and made swift progress into Mortain. But the overwhelming strength of American firepower, on the ground and in the air, stalled the advance. The fighting on Hill 317 was pivotal. Here the isolated 2nd Battalion of the 12th Infantry Regiment mounted a heroic defense. The 700-strong so-called "Lost Battalion" suffered nearly 300 killed or wounded, while each of the company commanders were awarded the Distinguished Service Cross (DSC).

The Germans sought to press home any advantage, but without the means to do so, the counterattack of "Operation Lüttich" failed. Mortain was laid waste by a withering American artillery bombardment, and by August 11, the Germans began what was to be a desperate attempt to escape or survive.

Chapter Fourteen:
Patton & Montgomery

"When I'm not attacking, I get bilious."
— George S. Patton

■ **LEFT:** With his ivory-handled revolver on his hip, Lieutenant-General George S. Patton Jr., sits on a hill while observing his troops rolling through the El Guettar Valley in Tunisia, during World War Two.

George S. Patton

If ever a commander had an apt nickname it was "Old Blood and Guts." George Smith Patton Jr. was the kind of man born for combat – on and off the battlefield. A mercurial, bombastic, bullying, eccentric, dynamic, reckless, inspiring, heroic, maddening, and brilliant commander, he was arguably the most compelling figure of the Normandy campaign. Even though he arrived late to the fighting, all eyes were on Patton once he was committed to battle.

Patton was a divisive figure: many of his men loved him, others among colleagues, subordinates, and superiors were antagonized by his uncompromising character. General Bradley was said to be overjoyed when he was promoted so that he could turn the tables on Patton and give the orders to his hitherto superior instead.

But whatever the complexities of Patton's character he seemed destined to lead. Born into a family with an illustrious military history, he graduated from West Point before competing in the 1912 Olympics in the Pentathlon. In World War One Patton was the first officer assigned to the Tank Corps. This early association with tanks was to have a profound effect on his career and he became a passionate advocate of mechanized armor in the inter-war years.

Promoted to major-general, he led the ground forces in Operation Torch, the invasion of northwest Africa in 1942, achieving decisive victory before leading the 7th Army to Sicily. The race with Montgomery to capture Palermo was an indication of Patton's drive and ego, and it soured their relationship. It was in Sicily where Patton struck a shell-shocked soldier, accusing him of cowardice. The incident contributed to Patton being effectively sidelined, until he was unleashed on the Germans in August 1944.

Released from his enforced inactivity like a cork out of a champagne bottle, Patton tore into the action, his 3rd Army sweeping across northern France in one of the greatest and fastest army advances in history. His disregard for convention served him well, and gained invaluable results for the Allies in the final push to defeat Germany. Indeed many Germans rated Patton as the best of the Allied commanders. As if fated not to last in a peacetime environment, he died shortly after a car accident in occupied Germany in December 1945.

Bernard Law Montgomery of Alamein, 1st Viscount

At most levels Patton and his sometime ally, often-time adversary, General Bernard Montgomery, seemed polar opposites. Where Patton was a physically confident commander who strutted with the air of an imposing man of action, Montgomery was a diminutive, slightly reedy figure who perhaps looked more like an office clerk rather than a battlefield warrior. Yet in Monty's leadership skills, ambition, arrogance, determined single-mindedness, and uneasy relationship with senior officers, the two had much in common.

"Monty," as he was almost universally known, came from a typical "officer-class' background of public school and the Royal Military College at Sandhurst. He joined the Royal Warwickshire Regiment and was injured while serving as a platoon leader. His experience as commander of the 3rd Division at Dunkirk provided important lessons, and by the time he was installed as the head of the 8th Army in North Africa in the summer of 1942, he arrived with a considerable burden on his shoulders.

The Allies desperately needed good news after three years of reverses. Churchill, enraged by the situation in the Middle East, demanded a general who could deliver victories. At El Alamein in October, Monty obliged. It was not a triumph of dashing tactics but testimony to Montgomery's ability to organize numerically superior forces, instill a vigorous fighting spirit, and restore morale. It was often said of Montgomery that he had a better relationship with the massed ranks than he did with staff officers, and Monty's slouch hat, caravan accommodation, and spartan lifestyle on the frontline endeared him to the foot soldiers if not senior officers more used to luxuries and strict class distinctions.

After success in Italy, Montgomery was brought back to England to head Allie land forces for the invasion of Normandy. His steady, cautious approach was informed by his wish to avoid the kind of slaughter he had witnessed in 1914-18, but it caused friction with many among his Allied colleagues, Patton chief among them. When Monty was more daring, it resulted in a rare defeat in the damaging disaster of the airborne landings at Arnhem.

Control of land forces was switched to General Eisenhower that month, a blow to Montgomery's standing and his ego. Nonetheless, promoted to field marshal, Montgomery remained in command of the 21st Army group and, after leading successful operations in Germany, he was at Luneburg Heath to take the surrender of the Nazis in May, 1945.

After the war, Montgomery was knighted and became a Viscount, commanding the British Army of the Rhine, and served as chief of the Imperial General Staff until 1948. In 1951, he became deputy commander of the Supreme Headquarters of the newly-formed NATO. He died on March 24, 1976.

"Indomitable in retreat, invincible in advance, insufferable in victory."
– **Winston Churchill on Montgomery**

■ **BELOW: Field Marshal Sir Bernard Montgomery won victory at El Alamein in World War Two, 1942; he helped plan the Normandy invasion.**

Chapter Fifteen:
The Falaise Gap

August 8 – August 20 **1944**

■ **ABOVE:** British and Canadian troops, having effectively closed the Falaise Gap, are pushing on toward the important communications center of Lisioux, and were reported to be only four miles from the town on August 20. During the advance British infantrymen were given a great welcome by the village of La Carneille.

With the failure of the German counterattack at Mortain, the position of Army Group B seemed irretrievable. The ability to oppose the thrust of American forces from the west was weakening almost hour by hour, while the position in the north against the British and Canadians was becoming increasingly precarious. Von Kluge simply did not have the means to mount an effective response. All that could be realistically planned for was a retreat and escape of almost Dunkirk proportions to the east in the hope of establishing a defensive line behind the Seine.

For the Allies, the opportunity for total victory was now clear. The original plan had been to outflank the Germans as far south as over the Loire but the collapse of German resistance presented the chance to squeeze the Germans via a rapid drive of Patton's 3rd Army by wheeling away from western Brittany toward Angers. For once there was near unanimity within Allied high command. "The main business is to the east," said Montgomery, though his attempt to claim the credit did a disservice to Bradley's decisiveness during Operation Cobra. "To hell with compromises," said Patton.

The German 7th Army – or what remained of its battered divisions – was effectively doomed. They were all-but trapped in a 20-mile bulge running west to east, with Falaise in the north and Argentan to the south forming a neck being throttled by twin Allied assaults.

In the north the Allies launched Operation Totalize with the newly activated Canadian 1st Army. While its tanks made initial headway, there was hesitancy in the follow-up by two divisions, compounded by a lack of support, and the advantage was not fully pressed home. German resistance may have been increasingly desperate but it was also viciously effective, and by August 11 the offensive stalled.

The contrast with the rapid movement of American forces to the south in previous days was marked, but here too, the attempt to close the gap was halted. Controversy persists over the decision to stop American columns heading further north, ostensibly to maintain discipline over the various sectors, but with the Canadians finally taking Falaise on August 16, the gap was reduced to 15 miles.

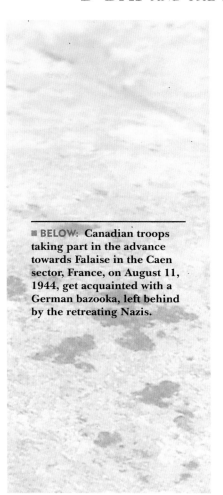

■ BELOW: **Canadian troops taking part in the advance towards Falaise in the Caen sector, France, on August 11, 1944, get acquainted with a German bazooka, left behind by the retreating Nazis.**

Over the next few days the noose was squeezed tighter as the Germans scrambled to escape, before US and Polish units joined up at Chambois on August 19. In the interim occurred one of the most infamous and savage battles of the war – a one-sided engagement that amounted to slaughter as much as combat. Men of the German 7th Army, joined by the 5th Panzer Army, choked the roads leading east in frenzied attempts to evade capture or annihilation. They presented easy targets for Allied artillery and aircraft.

The Germans fought ferociously to extricate themselves from the gap and inflicted severe punishment on isolated Allied positions, and up to 20,000 men may have escaped, but this was by any measure a catastrophic defeat. Precise numbers are hard to establish but upward of 10,000 Germans were killed, while 50,000 were taken prisoner. Even those who were able to flee left their

equipment behind. It is estimated that 500 tanks were knocked out or lost. Hundreds of artillery pieces suffered the same fate, while nearly 3,000 vehicles were destroyed.

Inside the gap was a hellish vision of mortality that never left the minds of combatants on either side. Trapped on narrow roads and attacked by artillery and Allied aircraft unhindered in their total command of the skies, whole columns of German troops were obliterated. Adding in the corpses of civilians, dead cattle, and the huge numbers of horses the Germans used to try and aid their flight, the whole area turned into a cesspit of death and decay. Dismembered bodies littered roadways and fragments of flesh hung from shattered branches. In the heat of August, flies proliferated in their millions, and the stench was unimaginable.

"It was literally possible to walk for hundreds of yards at a time, stepping on nothing but dead and decaying flesh."
– General Eisenhower

■ BELOW: **A line of German prisoners streams back from the area of Falaise, France on August 16, 1944, where they were captured by Allied troops, as Canadian tanks (rear) move forward to give support to advancing British forces.**

It was an apocalyptic scene. When Eisenhower visited the battlefield two days after it had been sealed, he was visibly taken aback, later recalling a "killing field" that "could be described only by Dante. It was literally possible to walk for hundreds of yards at a time, stepping on nothing but dead and decaying flesh."

The German army in the west had been crushed. Von Kluge had been ordered to return to Germany. Fearing the same retribution meted out to those officers suspected of undermining the Führer, von Kluge instead took his own life. It was one of the final acts of a momentous battle. It represented total victory for the western powers, and with both retreating Germans and the four Allied armies careering in a headlong race east to the Seine, Paris, and beyond, Operation Overlord was effectively at an end.

Chapter Sixteen:
Allied Air Power

When the Wehrmacht was cutting a swathe through Western Europe in 1940, the employment of blitzkrieg tactics was fundamental to German military success. Key to the impact of "lightning war" was the effective domination of the skies by the Luftwaffe. Four years later, as the Allies rolled back a dispirited and defeated German army in France, it was air power again that played a massive role in the outcome, this time with almost complete control of the air in American and British-led hands. The tables had not just been turned but completely overturned.

Both the use of strategic bombing of the German war machine by heavy bombers and the tactical deployment of fighters and fighter bombers over the Normandy battlefield were crucial in winning the campaign. Long before the invasion on June 6,

■ ABOVE: Because of the bubble-canopy, the pilot of this P-47 fighter bomber has no direct forward vision while the nose of the plane is up, so the crew chief and his assistant ride the wings of the plane from the parking place to the runway, somewhere in France, 1944, giving hand signals to guide the pilot.

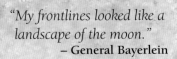

"My frontlines looked like a landscape of the moon."
– General Bayerlein

RAF and USAAF bombers had been pounding targets well behind the Atlantic Wall. Factories in the industrial heartlands of the Ruhr and elsewhere were destroyed, damaged, or hindered, with a debilitating effect on aircraft manufacture.

The lack of planes available to the Luftwaffe was due in part to the intensive bombing of German industry. Other factors came into play, such as the scale of the fighting on the Eastern Front draining already overstretched resources, and the withdrawal of Luftwaffe forces to defend Germany from the near constant attacks of RAF Bomber Command and the USA 8th Air Force. But there was also widespread resentment on the part of ground troops that the Luftwaffe had lost its collective nerve. A common complaint from embittered

soldiers was that pilots and Luftwaffe officers were guilty of cowardice. Whatever the reasons, such was Allied command of the air on D-Day itself that, as an illustration, only 36 Luftwaffe planes were identified over the British sector.

Without effective opposition, Allied planes were given free rein to wreak havoc across Normandy and beyond. Before D-Day, transport infrastructure was a vital target. RAF and USAAF planes bombed railway marshaling yards, forcing German supply efforts onto the cluttered roads. These in turn were attacked when the invasion began, hampering supply and reinforcement to Rommel's ground forces, and starving them of the means to fight effectively.

As ever, during the course of the war, disputes among senior commanders raged as to how air power could be best deployed, but

■ ABOVE: The RAF Typhoon is seen in flying formation. The single seater, low-wing monoplane is powered by a Napier Sabre engine and armed with either four cannons or 12 machine guns. Used both in night and day operations, the Typhoon is said to have been effective in attacking enemy trains, barges, and truck convoys, and even against trawlers and minesweepers.

the air strikes of Allied Expeditionary Air Forces (AEAF) could be devastating in their effectiveness. In the bombing raids that preceded the start of Operation Cobra, German troops and armor were almost annihilated. General Bayerlein of the Panzer Lehr Division said: "My frontlines looked like a landscape of the moon. At least 70% of my personnel were out of action – dead, wounded, crazed, or numbed."

As the advance progressed the co-ordination between forces on the ground and in the air improved to counter the threat of German armor, particularly among American units. The 9th Tactical Air Force, led by Major-General Elwood "Pete" Quesada, proved adept in this regard. Quesada's forces in the last week of July claimed to have destroyed over 360 tanks. Even allowing for exaggeration,

the effect was enormous.

Allied planes could lay waste to targets and prepare the ground for the movement of armor. Tank commanders would radio for P-47 Thunderbolts to pinpoint columns of tanks and even single guns. At Mortain, it was the entry of RAF Typhoons that was a major factor in stopping the German counterattack.

Armed with racks of eight rockets boasting 60 pounds of high explosive, the Typhoons of the RAF's 83 Group attacked a column of the 1st SS Panzer Division on August 7. Flying in rotation, they presented a conveyor belt of near constant air assault, their rockets screaming in on the exposed column. When the rockets had been fired, the planes returned to strafe with 20mm cannon.

While the claims for the accuracy of the Typhoons' attacks were greatly exaggerated, they were highly effective. They tied up German armor, prevented their deployment against ground troops, and caused panic among the Germans. Many tank crews would flee, rendering their abandoned vehicles as useless as ones

actually destroyed. The mere presence of Allied planes was pivotal, wearing down morale and striking fear into any German who heard the drone of air engines.

This was a feature no more evident than in the Falaise Gap. With so many troops and armor packed into such a small area, it became something of a turkey shoot for Allied aircrew who flew up to 12,000 sorties. While the claims for the destruction of tanks through rocket or bombing runs were again overplayed, air attacks destroyed what was left of meager fuel supplies, precipitated panic among fleeing troops, and proved horrifically effective against "soft-skinned" vehicles, along with defeated troops marching on foot in the increasingly futile hope of escape. The charnel-house scene of the gap was caused in significant part by the brutally effective and ill-matched engagement between powerful modern aircraft and soldiers armed with little more than rifles and diminishing rounds of ammunition. It was a one-way fight with only one outcome.

■ BELOW: **German tanks and transport wrecked by rocket-firing Typhoons of the RAF in France.**

Chapter Seventeen:
The Liberation of Paris

August 19 – August 25 1944

■ **ABOVE:** Adolf Hitler is shown here with other German officials walking in front of the Eiffel Tower in Paris, France, in 1940.

On June 28, 1940, Adolf Hitler posed for photos in front of the Eiffel Tower with Albert Speer, the "Third Reich's Architect" in chief, along with a horde of officers and acolytes. But for the military uniforms, it might have looked like a group of tourists taking in the sights of the French capital. Except it was the most infamous figure in history in triumphant mood after reviewing one of his most prized conquests, and a disturbing symbol of the Nazis' quest for world domination.

Four years later, there was a quite different scene. Jubilant Parisians thronged the boulevards and streets welcoming their freedom as Free French soldiers drove down the Champs Elysees on an emotional journey of redemption.

The road to Paris from the Normandy beaches had been bloody, and even with the German 7th Army in a tailspin and the Allies in concerted pursuit, fighting was still costly for both sides. Enough Wehrmacht troops had escaped to render the German retreat a fighting one, particularly on the British and Canadian advance to the lower Seine where there were a series of brutal small-scale actions.

However, Operation Anvil, renamed Dragoon, to invade Vichy France on the Mediterranean coast, had been launched on August 15 and made rapid progress. With the Germans in retreat on all fronts the war was entering its decisive phase – but the race to the Seine was the focus of attention.

The jostling for position and power increased. A glittering prize of a major European capital was now in sight, and not only were there continuing disputes between senior American and British commanders, but also the Free French forces. General Charles de Gaulle had been, to the Allies' intense irritation, constantly maneuvering for influence,

demanding control of aspects of military operations while pursuing a political agenda with the destiny of post-war France in mind. In turn, De Gaulle and his officers suspected that they were being sidelined by the "Anglo-Saxon" alliance of Americans and British. Factoring in communist-led opposition to De Gaulle within the Resistance and among Parisians themselves, it meant that the battle took on the appearance of a single objective

■ ABOVE: A Sherman tank of the French Armored Division passes by the Arc de Triomphe during the final hours of the struggle to liberate the French capital from German occupation, August 1944.

being fought on multiple fronts.

The Resistance had played a vital part during the Normandy campaign, aiding special operatives, sabotaging transport links, and harrying German forces on the frontline and in the rear. Now they seized their opportunity for more overt action, fueled by revenge for the dreadful injustices of four years of occupation. A general strike began on August 18. A day later, at the same time as Patton's forward units reached the Seine, the Paris uprising began.

"People are giving us flowers, tomatoes, it's just been the most marvellous procession I have ever seen... they're just mad with joy."
– the BBC's Robert Reid on the day of Paris' liberation

■ **ABOVE:** Thousands of Parisians in carnival mood thronged the streets of their city in Paris, on August 26, 1944, to cheer General de Gaulle as he marched from the Arc de Triomphe to the Place de la Concorde.

Communist posters appeared calling for an armed uprising, signed by Henri Rol Tanguy, the leader of the Resistance in the Ile de France. The uneasy truce agreed by the Swedish consul-general, Raoul Nordling, with the German commander of the Paris garrison, Generalleutnant von Choltitz, was broken by sporadic skirmishes and firefights that developed into more intense action. The situation was on a knife-edge ,but with the cry of "Toux aus barricades!" the Resistance became emboldened and closed in on the garrison, now holed up in the center of the city.

On August 22, groups of Germans began to attempt an escape. By August 25, many of the soldiers who had been ordered by Hitler to defend Paris to their last drop of blood, had slipped away under cover of darkness. American and French forces had made their way into the center of the capital taking casualties but avoiding the kind of slaughter some had feared.

Amid recriminations over De Gaulle's conduct and accusations over a lack of recognition for the Americans, it was left to the Free French 2nd Armored Division, led by General Philippe Leclerc, to take the surrender of von Choltitz. The generalleutnant had been having lunch with his staff at the Hotel Meurice, their meal interrupted by small arms fire that shattered windows and brought down plaster on their table.

The reaction was suitably emotional. Ernest Hemingway, a figure much derided by some war correspondents, was on the scene and reflected that "I had a funny choke in my throat and I had to clean my glasses because there now, below us, gray and always beautiful, was spread the city I love best in all the world." Hundreds of thousands wept with relief and happiness. Others sought violent retribution against unarmed German prisoners and suspected collaborators, guilty or otherwise.

Paris was in Allied hands, but the fighting in the capital was not yet over, as sniper fire continued from remaining fanatical German soldiers, joined by French Fascists. And on the same day, elsewhere in still occupied France, SS soldiers were still committing atrocities. The war was not yet over.

■ **BELOW:** A group of Paris civilians read the news of the liberation of their city in *France Libre*, a Paris newspaper, on August 26, 1944.

Chapter Eighteen:
The Aftermath of the Battle

August 25 **1944** – May **1945**

"There was a man tending to a soldier who... was obviously dead. And I remember the other lad saying: 'He can't be dead. I promised his mother I'd look after him.' It struck me then that there was something wrong with that. I could quite happily have put my rifle down."

– Private Dennis Brown, 5th Battalion, East Yorkshire Regiment

Joseph Goebbels' demand in 1943 for total war would play its sickening cameo in the deaths of millions more men, women, and children. The fighting was far from over in France, likewise in Italy, the Pacific, Asia, and in Eastern Europe. After Allied victory in Normandy, many more young men in uniform – and innocent civilians – would pay the ultimate price for total war.

One man who had already joined the growing roll call of death was Michael Wittmann, the SS tank commander whose exploits in destroying units of the British 7th Armoured Division at Villers-Bocage had helped create his legend. Wittmann was killed on August 8, when his Tiger tank was blown up, probably by Trooper Joe Ekins of the 1st Northamptonshire Yeomanry, during Operation Totalize.

Wittmann's compatriots, however, would inflict further bloody damage on Allied forces after Paris' liberation. That there was enough in the way of intact German forces able to wage a fighting retreat caused huge controversy, particularly over the Falaise Gap. Had the gap been closed earlier and the German 7th Army been defeated even more comprehensively, the war may not have dragged on for almost another year. But that was just one of several possible consequences and "what ifs."

The reality was that Montgomery's objectives to reach the Seine had been achieved with 10 days to spare. The initial invasion, the grind of wearing down German armor around Caen, the physical and psychological torments of the "battle of the bocage," and the ferocity of 11 weeks of intense warfare wrote a grim chapter in 20th-century history. The fighting in

■ **LEFT: Montgomery stands in his car as he is driven over a Bailey bridge across the River Seine at Vernon, France, on September 8, 1944.**

63

Normandy was horrendous. In places it could match the Eastern Front for its savagery and at times was as costly as the slaughter of the Western Front in World War One. Yet Overlord was a success.

Montgomery had acknowledgment of his achievement with promotion to field marshal in September, even if his standing with Allied command was actually reduced. Eisenhower had proved to be an adept supreme commander in gaining agreement and purpose, Bradley and Patton similarly on the frontline. Their troops, many of them untested "Doughboys," had shown what effective and courageous fighting men they were, along with a

multitude of combatants from other nations joined in the Allied cause. The war-weary British "Tommy" demonstrated he still had plenty of fight left in him. But so too did the soldiers of the Wehrmacht. It was all at a terrible cost.

Seventy years on from the summer of 1944, it is still hard to pinpoint exact casualty figures, but estimates for the civilian population account for up to 30,000 dead, many incurred as a result of Allied bombing. Allied military figures are estimated at over 83,000 for the British-Canadian-Polish 21st Army group – including 16,000 killed and 9,000 missing – and 126,000 for the Americans,

of which nearly 21,000 were fatal. Combining air force losses, the total Allied casualties amount to around a quarter of a million.

Quantifying German losses is more confusing, given the turmoil of Nazi operations, but it is believed up to 240,000 were killed and wounded, and in excess of 200,000 captured.

Over 40 German divisions were destroyed, with a catastrophic consequence for the Axis powers. Hitler's megalomaniacal plan for a new world order dominated by the Third Reich was not yet in ruins but D-Day and the battle for Normandy had played a major part in ensuring it would never be realized.

Sources:

Bailey, R., *Forgotten Voices: D-Day* (Ebury Press, 2009)

Beevor, A., *D-Day The Battle For Normandy* (Penguin, 2012)

D'Este, C., *Decision In Normandy: The Real Story of Montgomery and the Allied Campaign* (Penguin, 2001)

Gilbert, M., *D-Day* (John Wylie, 2004)

Dictionary of 20th Century World Biography (OUP, 1992)

BBC

ddaymuseum.co.uk

wikipedia

Linked

INNOVATIVE CHAIN MAIL
JEWELRY DESIGNS

Featuring
John Fetvedt
Diane Miller
Anne Mitchell
Laura Poplin
Sue Ripsch
Vanessa Walilko

Compiled by
Karin Van Voorhees

KALMBACH BOOKS

Kalmbach Books
21027 Crossroads Circle
Waukesha, Wisconsin 53186
www.Kalmbach.com/Books

Lettered step-by-step photos pages 6–16 by Sue Ripsch, pages 25–26 by Diane Miller, page 29 by Kate Ferrant Richbourg, pages 37–38 by Anne Mitchell and Kate Ferrant Richbourg, page 41–45 by John Fetvedt, and pages 61–72 by Laura Poplin. All other photography © 2014 Kalmbach Books.

Published in 2014
18 17 16 15 14   1 2 3 4 5

Manufactured in China

ISBN: 978-1-62700-089-5
EISBN: 978-1-62700-080-2

The material in this book has appeared previously in *Bead&Button, Art Jewelry,* or *Wirework* magazines or *Unconventional Chain Mail Jewelry* or *Classic Chain Mail Jewelry* books. *Bead&Button, Art Jewelry,* and *Wirework* are registered as trademarks.

Editor: Karin Van Voorhees
Art Director: Carole Ross
Photographers: William Zuback and James Forbes

Publisher's Cataloging-in-Publication Data

Linked : innovative chain mail jewelry designs / compiled by
  Karin Van Voorhees.

    p. : col. ill. ; cm.

  "Featuring John Fetvedt, Diane Miller, Anne Mitchell, Laura Poplin, Sue Ripsch, Vanessa Walilko."
  "The material in this book has appeared previously in *Bead&Button*, *Art Jewelry*, or *Wirework* magazines or *Unconventional Chain Mail Jewelry* or *Classic Chain Mail Jewelry books*."—T.p. verso.
    Issued also as an ebook.
    ISBN: 978-1-62700-089-5

  1. Chains (Jewelry)—Handbooks, manuals, etc. 2. Metal-work—Handbooks, manuals, etc. 3. Jewelry making—Handbooks, manuals, etc. I. Van Voorhees, Karin.

TT212 .L565 2014
745.594/2

contents

SUE RIPSCH

DIANE MILLER

ANNE MITCHELL

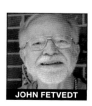
JOHN FETVEDT

VANESSA WALILKO

LAURA POPLIN

Ancient Art for Modern Times

Centuries ago, chain mail (or maille) armor was created by the Celtic people for solely practical purposes. Tightly linked metal rings provided unprecedented protection on the battlefield—a distinct advantage to those who wore it.

Linking tiny rings of gold, silver, or steel progressed from purely utilitarian purposes, and chain mail jewelry and other adornments became common. Chain mail weaves evolved from three distinct cultures: Japanese, known for using small rings in flat patterns such as the 12-in-2 or the Chrysanthemum; European, most commonly recognized for the 4-in-1 pattern and its variations; and Persian, distinguished by more decorative ornamentation.

Contemporary chain mail artists have not only reproduced ancient weaves, but they also have combined and blended patterns and materials into unique, modern jewelry art. Six such artists are featured in this collection: Sue Ripsch, Diane Miller, Anne Mitchell, John Fetvedt, Vanessa Walilko, and Laura Poplin. Each designer opens, links, and closes jump rings with the same motions, but the resulting jewelry couldn't be more different. Whether it's gleaming sterling silver chain that flows along the wrist, bold and colorful combinations of anodized niobium links, or patterned chain blended with organic leather or sparkling crystal, you are sure to find projects in this collection that challenge your creativity and boost your understanding of this remarkable art.

Before you begin, you may want to review the Basics section beginning on page 73. You'll find a thorough explanation of tools used in chain mail, an overview of different metals and how they fare in jump ring and chain mail construction, and comprehensive directions for making your own jump rings. Additionally, basic instructions for soldering, finishing, and jewelry-making techniques are included. Finally, experts Vanessa Walilko and Anne Mitchell provide excellent commentary on chain mail standards and practices, and on using aspect ratio to control the fit of a piece.

Sue Ripsch

"Chain mail allows creative expression and results in fine, handmade jewelry."

A registered nurse by profession, Sue has always enjoyed handcrafts. When she took a class to learn Byzantine weave, she became hooked on chain mail. She worked from whatever scarce patterns she could find and soon began developing her own designs. As she began to teach others, she realized that she wanted to share her knowledge and instructions with as many people as she could by writing books. She is honored to join you in your creative pursuits and hopes she adds a small amount of joy to your life.

3-in-3 with a Twist
chain & earrings

Simple but elegant, the twisted rings in this set give off a beautiful radiance and shine that draws the eye to your wrist or ears. The bracelet is substantial but lies nicely along your wrist and is quite comfortable to wear.

a

b

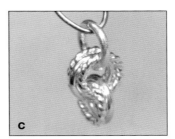

c

d

materials

bracelet, 7 in. (18cm)
- Sterling silver jump rings
  - **70** 16-gauge 5.0mm ID, 10 rings per in. (4 rings per cm)
  - **70** 16-gauge 5.0mm ID twisted, 10 rings per in. (4 rings per cm)
  - **2** 16-gauge 5.0mm ID
- Clasp

earrings
- Sterling silver jump rings
  - **14** 16-gauge 5.0mm ID
  - **12** 16-gauge 5.0mm ID twisted
- Pair of earring wires

tools
- Chainnose pliers
- Flatnose pliers
- Wire tie

Jump rings and kits for Sue's projects are available from jewelrybysueonline.com

e

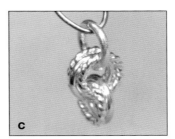

f

Bracelet

[1] Close two twisted rings and one smooth ring, and open one smooth ring. Continue opening rings throughout the pattern as needed.

[2] With the open ring, pick up a closed twisted ring, a closed smooth ring, and a closed twisted ring. Close the open ring. Run a wire tie through the single closed ring and twist the ends of the wire closed. You have a 1-3 chain **(a)**.

[3] Run an open smooth ring through the three rings and close the ring. You now have a 1-3-1 chain **(b)**.

[4] Run an open twisted ring through the three rings alongside the last ring added and close the ring. You now have a 1-3-2 chain **(c)**.

[5] Run an open smooth ring through the three rings alongside the last ring added so the twisted ring is between the two smooth rings. Close the ring. You now have a 1-3-3 chain **(d)**.

Notice how the first set of three rings is composed of a twisted-smooth-twisted ring combination, and the second set of three rings is a smooth-twisted-smooth combination. You will alternate these two combinations throughout the length of the bracelet.

[6] Build the chain to the desired length. Continue adding rings as in steps 3–5, alternating the two-ring combinations.

[7] On each end of the chain, use a single ring to attach the clasp **(e)**.

Change the ring combination, using all smooth rings or all twisted rings, or even making the bracelet two-tone if desired. Remember that the chain uses almost seven sets of three rings per inch in whatever combination of rings chosen.

Earrings

[1] Follow steps 1–5 of the bracelet instructions. You will have a 1-3-3 chain in an alternating combination of twisted-smooth-twisted and smooth-twisted-smooth rings.

[2] Repeat steps 3–6 of "Bracelet" until you have a 1-3-3-3-3 chain in the alternating sets of three rings as in the bracelet instructions.

[3] Remove the wire tie. Open the ring that was on the wire and run it through the loop in an earring finding. Close the ring **(f)**. Repeat steps 1–3 to make a second earring.

Make the earrings longer or shorter by adding or removing additional sets of three rings to the chain.

Celtic Line
bracelet & earrings

The Celtic Line bracelet has an Irish feel to it. The jump rings form circles within circles that are stylish and appealing. A great everyday piece of jewelry, the Celtic Line bracelet is attractive and comfortable.

materials

bracelet, 7 in. (18cm)
- Sterling silver jump rings
  - **56** 18-gauge 6.0mm ID, 8 rings per in. (4 rings per cm)
  - **42** 18-gauge 3.5mm ID, 6 rings per in. (3 rings per cm)
- Clasp

earrings
- Sterling silver jump rings
  - **16** 18-gauge 6.0mm ID, 8 rings per in. (4 rings per cm)
  - **14** 18-gauge 3.5mm ID, 6 rings per in. (3 rings per cm), plus 2 connector rings
- Pair of earring wires

tools
- Chainnose pliers
- Flatnose pliers
- Wire tie

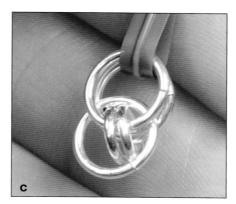

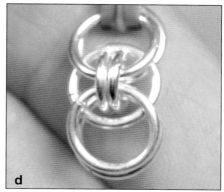

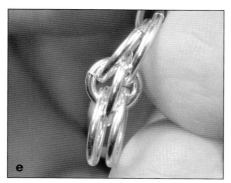

Bracelet

[1] Close two large rings. Run a wire tie through the rings and twist the ends of the wire closed **(a)**. Open a pile of small rings and a pile of large rings. Open rings as needed throughout the pattern.

[2] Run an open small ring through the previous two large rings and close the ring. Run another open small ring through the same path. Close the ring **(b)**.

[3] Run an open large ring between the two large rings and around the two small rings. Close the ring **(c)**. Note that this large ring does not go through any rings, but rather around and between rings. I call this a "floater" ring.

[4] Run an open large ring through the two small end rings, being sure that the large ring is lying on top of the floater ring **(d)**.

[5] Turn the chain over and repeat step 4 on the other side of the floater ring. The floater ring is sandwiched between two sets of two large rings **(e)**.

[6] Repeat step 2–5 **(f)** until the chain is the desired length. Attach your clasp to each end, placing two small rings through the two end large rings and the clasp.

Earrings

[1] Weave a 1-in. (2.5cm) piece of chain following the bracelet instructions. End the chain with step 5. Attach the chain to an earring wire with two small rings **(g)**.

[2] Make a second earring.

Make the earrings any desired length by adding or subtracting rings.

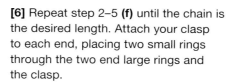

Crazy Eight
set

A wonderful combination of color and silver, this original weave has trapped crystals within a cage of rings. I named the weave Crazy Eight because the crystal segments resemble the number eight and the rolling rings add a crazy touch to the chain.

materials

bracelet, 7 in. (18cm)

- Sterling silver jump rings
  - **72** 18-gauge 6.0mm ID, 8 rings per in. (4 rings per cm)
  - **7** 18-gauge 3.0mm ID
  - **7** 18-gauge 4.2 x 6.5mm ID oval
  - **21** 12-gauge 6.5mm ID, 3 rings per in. (2 rings per cm)
- **12** 6mm round crystals
- Clasp

necklace, 40 in. (102cm)

- Sterling silver jump rings
  - **312** 18-gauge 6.0mm ID, 8 rings per in. (4 rings per cm)
  - **39** 18-gauge 3.0mm ID
  - **39** 18-gauge 4.2 x 6.5mm ID oval
  - **117** 12-gauge 6.5mm ID, 3 rings per in. (2 rings per cm)
- **78** 6mm round crystals
- Clasp

earrings

- Sterling silver jump rings
  - **16** 18-gauge 6.0mm ID
  - **4** 18-gauge 3.0mm ID
  - **2** 22-gauge 2.0mm ID
- **4** 6mm round crystals
- Pair of earring wires

Use round crystals, as other shapes (such as bicones) may fall through the cage.

tools

- Chainnose pliers
- Flatnose pliers
- Wire tie

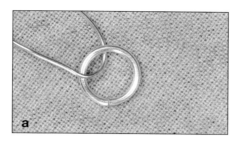

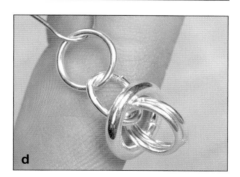

Bracelet and necklace

[1] Open nine 18-gauge 6.0mm rings and one oval ring. Close a 6.0mm ring and place it on a wire tie. Twist the end of the wire closed **(a)**.

[2] Run an open oval ring through the end ring and close the ring **(b)**.

The oval rings do not always close with as nice a join as a round ring, but do not worry too much about that. The oval ring will be surrounded with 12-gauge rings, and the join will not show.

[3] Run an open 6.0mm ring through the oval ring and close the ring. Run a second 6.0mm ring through the same path and close the ring. You now have a 1-1-2 chain **(c)**.

[4] Open a 12-gauge ring and run it around the oval ring. Close the ring **(d)**. (The new ring fits around the oval and does not fall off the end of the chain because the 6.0mm rings block it.)

[5] Repeat step 4 with two more 12-gauge rings **(e)**. As you are placing these rings, keep pulling the oval ring so it lies lengthwise between the 18-gauge rings on each of its ends. The oval will try to slip sideways, so continue to adjust it until you have all three 12-gauge rings on and closed.

f

g

h

i

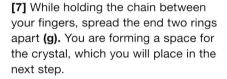

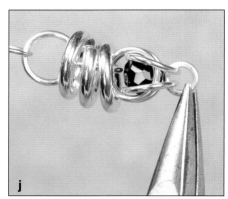

j

k

[6] Run two open 6.0mm rings through the two end rings, closing each ring as you go **(f).** Open a 3.0mm ring and place it on your mat.

[7] While holding the chain between your fingers, spread the end two rings apart **(g).** You are forming a space for the crystal, which you will place in the next step.

[8] Spread the two inside rings apart and place a round crystal in the space formed by the four rings **(h)**. Hold the rings and crystal in place with your fingers. You may need to pull the last two rings so they lie one on each side of the connecting oval ring where it is attached to the first two 6.0mm rings.

[9] Run the open 3.0mm ring from your mat through the two end rings **(i)**. Close the ring. The crystal is now trapped in the four-ring cage **(j)**.

[10] Run two 6.0mm rings through the 3.0mm ring on the end. Run two more 6.0mm rings through the two end rings **(k)**.

[11] Repeat steps 7–8, trapping another crystal. Repeat step 9, using an open oval ring **(l)** instead of the 3.0mm ring. The pattern is now beginning to repeat.

[12] As you did in step 3, run two 6.0mm rings through the oval ring **(m)**. Repeat the pattern from steps 7–13, forming another crystal segment and another oval ring segment. Then add three of the 12-gauge rings as in steps 5–6. Continue repeating these steps for the length of the chain.

[13] When the chain is the desired length, remove the wire tie and attach one half of your clasp on that end by opening the end ring and running it through the clasp **(n)**.

For a lobster claw clasp, use the end ring to clasp the piece. For a toggle, attach the second half of the clasp to the remaining end ring.

Earrings

[1] Open eight 6.0mm rings, two 3.0mm rings, and one 2.0mm ring.

[2] Run a 3.0mm ring through the earring finding loop and close the ring **(o)**.

[3] Run a 6.0mm ring through the end ring and close the ring. Run a second ring through the same path and close the ring **(p)**.

[4] Run a 6.0mm ring through the pair of 6.0mm rings and close it. Repeat with a second 6.0mm ring. You now have a 1-2-2 chain **(q)**.

[5] Follow steps 7–10 in "Bracelet and Necklace."

[6] Follow steps 7–9, using a 2.0mm ring instead of a 3.0mm ring in step 10 to close the end of the earrings **(r)**. Make a second earring.

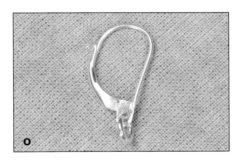

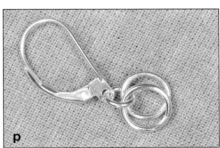

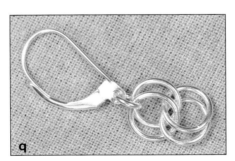

Monty Python bracelet

This original design is a wonderful complement to your jewelry collection. This bracelet reminds me of the undulations of a snake— it is really remarkable how it seems to flow along the wrist.

materials

bracelet, 7 in. (18cm)
- Sterling silver jump rings
  - **24** 16-gauge 6.7mm ID, 4 rings per segment
  - **48** 18-gauge 5.5mm ID, 8 rings per segment
  - **48** 20-gauge 5.0mm ID, 8 rings per segment
  - **28** 22-gauge 3.6mm ID, 4 rings per segment plus 4 rings for the end of the bracelet
- Clasp

Each segment is longer than 1 in. (2.5cm).

tools
- Chainnose pliers
- Flatnose pliers
- Wire tie

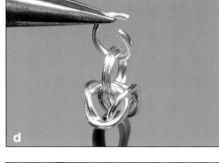

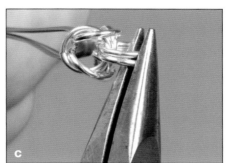

[1] Build a chain segment. Open and lay in individual piles of four rings each: 22-gauge rings, 20-gauge rings, 18-gauge rings, 16-gauge rings, 18-gauge rings, 20-gauge rings, and 22-gauge rings. These 28 rings represent one full segment of the bracelet. Close two of the 22-gauge rings and place them on a wire tie. Run an open 22-gauge ring through the first two rings and close the ring. Repeat with a second ring to make a 2–2 chain **(a)**. This will use all four rings in the first pile of 22-gauge rings. As you build the bracelet, use the sizes of rings in groups of four in the order stated earlier in this step.

[2] Build the bracelet chain. Flip the top two rings down, split the next pair of rings, and place an open ring between the split rings and through the bottom edge of the two flipped rings (which are now on top) **(b)**. Close the ring. Run another ring through the same path and close it **(c)**.

[3] Place a ring through the top two rings. Do not close the ring yet **(d)**.

[4] Before closing, twist the ring around and run it through the two rings of the downward-pointing V, or toward the wire tie **(e)**. Close the ring.

[5] Turn the segment over so that you see the downward-pointing V on the other side of the chain. Run another open ring through the top two rings. Again before closing, twist the ring around and run it through the two rings of the downward-pointing V on the opposite side of the segment. Close the ring **(f)**.

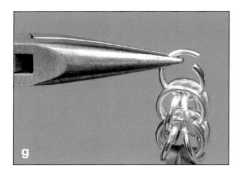

[6] Split the top two rings and place an open ring through the two rings in the center of the split rings **(g)**. Close the ring. Run another ring through the same path **(h)**. Once you have used all of the rings in the piles, the first segment is complete **(i)**.

[7] Repeat step 1 to build another segment, using the last set of 22-gauge rings from the first segment as the beginning set of rings for the next segment; you will weave a set of four rings onto the first segment in each size going in this order: 20-gauge, 18-gauge, 16-gauge, 18-gauge, 20-gauge, and 22-gauge.

[8] Continue building segments as instructed until the chain reaches the desired length **(j)**. Remove the wire tie. To attach the clasp, run two 20-gauge rings through the rings at one end of the chain and through one half of the clasp. Repeat on the other end of the bracelet with the other half of the clasp.

Luxurious length
Easily make a necklace by adding segments until you reach the desired length.

Diane Miller

Diane Miller lives in Wisconsin with her husband and loves everything about jewelry making; she now focuses on the intricate work of handcrafting different sized jump rings and designing unique new chain mail kits. When Diane is not teaching chain mail classes or selling her finished jewelry at art fairs throughout Southeastern Wisconsin, she enjoys taking long bike rides, visiting with family and friends, and traveling to warm tropical locations.

Celtic Visions
pendant

Craft a shiny pendant with jump rings in four sizes, and use a bail to attach your pendant to a piece of leather or rubber cord. For many, this piece evokes the complexity of a Celtic knot. What vision do you see?

materials

pendant, 1 in. (25.5cm)

- Sterling silver jump rings
  - **15** 16-gauge (1.3mm), 7.0mm ID
  - **1** 16-gauge (1.3mm), 5.5mm ID
  - **26** 16-gauge (1.3mm), 4.0mm ID
- Bail

tools

- **2** pairs of chainnose, bentnose, or flatnose pliers
- Needle tool or pick

Kits for all of Diane's projects are available at www.midwestmaille.com.

[1] Close one 5.5mm jump ring **(a)**. Open all remaining rings.

[2] Slide a 4mm ring through the closed 5.5mm ring, and close it. Repeat to attach nine more 4mm rings to the closed 5.5mm ring **(b)**.

[3] Slide a 7mm ring through two of the 4mm rings, and close it **(c)**. Repeat to attach four more 7mm rings to pairs of 4mm rings **(d)**

[4] Slide a 4mm ring through two 7mm rings, and close it. Repeat four times to connect all the 7mm rings **(e)**.

[5] Slide a 7mm ring through two of the 4mm rings. Make sure the 4mm jump rings you added in step 4 are sitting in the middle of the new 7mm jump ring you just added. Add four more 7mm jump rings the same way. Close the rings **(f)**.

[6] Turn the piece over, and repeat step 5 on this side **(g)**.

[7] Slide a 4mm ring through all three layers of 7mm rings, passing it through the "eye" formed where the two outer layers intersect the inner layer. Close the ring. Repeat nine times **(h)**.

[8] Slide a 4mm ring through a pair of 4mm rings and a bail, and close it **(i)**. String the pendant as desired.

Vortex
pendant & earrings

Spin a few jump rings into a whirling spiral of silver that makes a perfect pair of earrings or a simple pendant.

materials

pendant, 1⅛ in. (29mm)
- Argentium sterling silver jump rings, 16-gauge (1.29mm)
  - **10** 9mm ID
  - **2** 5.5mm ID
  - **1** 3.5mm ID
- Sterling silver bail

earrings
- Argentium sterling silver jump rings, 18-gauge (1.02mm)
  - **14** 6mm ID
  - **6** 4mm ID
- Pair of sterling silver earring findings

tools
- **2** pairs of chainnose, bentnose, or flatnose pliers
- Needle tool or pick

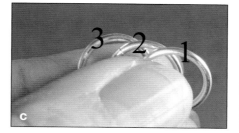

Pendant

[1] Close a 9mm jump ring and open nine 9mm jump rings. Open two 5.5mm jump rings and one 3.5mm jump ring.

[2] Slide a 9mm jump ring through the closed 9mm ring, and close it. Slide the two jump rings together so the top of ring 2 is behind ring 1 **(a)**.

[3] Add a 9mm ring through the center of the first two rings, and close it **(b)**. Slide ring 3 into position behind ring 2 **(c)**.

[4] Add a fourth 9mm ring through the center of the first three rings **(d)**, and close it. Position the fourth ring behind jump ring 3 **(e)**.

[5] Follow the same pattern to add six more 9mm rings **(f)**.

[6] One at a time, insert the 5.5mm rings through the center of the vortex, and close them. Slide the 3.5mm ring through the 5.5mm rings and through a bail finding. Close the ring **(g)**.

Earrings

[1] Close one 6mm jump ring, and open six 6mm jump rings. Open three 4mm jump rings.

[2] Using 6mm jump rings, follow steps 2–5 of the pendant to make a vortex.

[3] One at a time, insert two 4mm rings through the center of the vortex, and close them. Slide the remaining 4mm ring through the two 4mm rings you just added and through the loop of an earring wire. Close the ring **(h)**. Repeat to make a second earring.

Queen's Link
bracelet

Craft a flexible, heavy box chain using cost-savvy sterling silver-plated jump rings. The shining finished bracelet looks and wears just like sterling, but at a prettier price.

materials

bracelet, 7¾ x ½ in. (197x13mm)

- Sterling silver-plated jump rings
  - **66** 16-gauge (1.3mm), 6mm ID (large)
  - **64** 18-gauge (1.0mm), 5mm ID (medium)

tools

- 2 pairs of chainnose, bentnose, or flatnose pliers
- Needle tool or pick

[1] Open all of the jump rings. Create a 2-in-2-in-2 chain using four large rings and two medium rings (shown in pink). Slide the two medium jump rings in the center, through four closed large rings **(a)**. Close the ring.

[2] Squeeze the two large end rings of the chain between your fingers. Separate the second pair of large rings, positioning one on your index finger and the other on your thumb. The two medium rings are now on top **(b)**.

[3] Fold back the two large end rings and hold them between your finger and thumb. Separate the medium top rings to expose the two large rings folded back in step 2 **(c)**.

[4] One at a time, slide two medium rings through this opening, sliding through the tops of the two large rings exposed in step 3 **(d)**. Close the rings.

[5] One at a time, slide two large rings through the two medium rings added in step 4 **(e)**. Close the rings.

[6] Holding the chain in your hand, separate and fold back the two large rings added in step 5 **(f)**.

[7] Fold down the two large rings and hold them between your finger and thumb. Separate the medium top rings to expose the pair of large rings folded back in step 6 **(g)**.

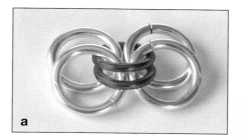

a

b

c

d

e

f

g

h

[8] Repeat steps 4–7 until the chain reaches the desired length. Remember to include the clasp measurement when calculating the overall length **(h)**.

[9] Slide a medium ring and the toggle clasp loop through two rings on the end of the chain and close the ring **(i)**. On the opposite end of the chain, slide two medium rings through the two large end rings. Close the rings. Slide a second pair of medium rings through the two previous rings. Slide one medium ring and the toggle bar through the last two rings and close the ring **(j)**.

i

j

GSG
Chain Mail
bracelet

GSG is short for "Great Southern Gathering," an event produced by the Society for Creative Anachronism, an international organization dedicated to researching and re-creating the arts and skills of pre-17th-century Europe. This weave, established at the event, is related to Persian sheet weaves. It may look complicated, but it goes together quickly once you get the hang of the pattern.

materials

bracelet, 7½ in. (19.1cm)
- Argentium sterling silver jump rings, 16-gauge (1.29mm)
  - **108** 6mm ID
  - **4** 4mm ID
- Clasp

tools

- **2** pairs of chainnose, bentnose, or flatnose pliers
- Needle tool or pick
- Twist tie

[1] Close two 6mm rings, and open 106. Slide the two closed rings onto an open ring, and close it. Arrange so the two closed rings overlap and the one you strung them on goes through the space created where they overlap **(a)**.

[2] Insert a twist tie up through ring 2 and down through ring 1, leaving a loop between the rings. The twist tie will keep the end rings in the correct position, and the loop will identify the front of your chain **(b)**. Always work with the front of the chain facing you.

[3] Flip ring 3 to the left **(c)**.

[4] Insert a ring (4) through the center of rings 1 and 2, and close it **(d)**.

[5] Insert a ring (5) through the space created where rings 3 and 4 overlap, and close it. Flip the new ring to the left **(e)**.

[6] Insert a ring (6) through the centers of rings 3 and 4, and close it **(f)**.

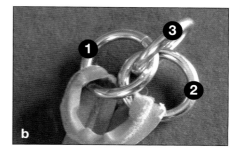

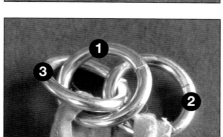

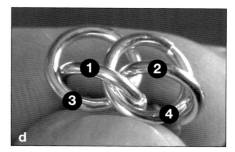

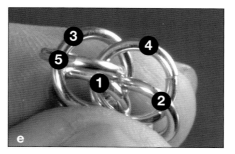

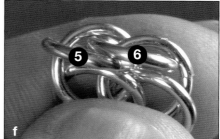

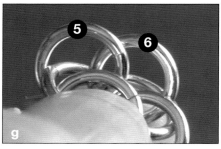

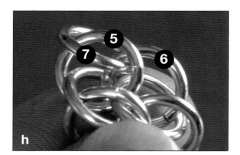

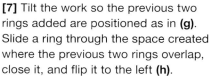

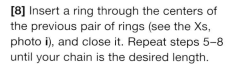

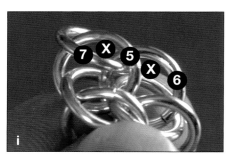

[7] Tilt the work so the previous two rings added are positioned as in **(g)**. Slide a ring through the space created where the previous two rings overlap, close it, and flip it to the left **(h)**.

[8] Insert a ring through the centers of the previous pair of rings (see the Xs, photo **i**), and close it. Repeat steps 5–8 until your chain is the desired length.

[9] Insert a 4mm ring through the space created where an end pair of rings overlap, attach half of the clasp, and close the ring. Repeat at the other end of the chain.

Anne Mitchell

"My goal is to try to learn something new every day I spend in my studio."

Anne was the first instructor to teach ancient chain mail patterns on the national level. She discovered metalwork through an art book from a museum gift shop that depicted images of chain mail patterns throughout history. She began deciphering the intricacies of any mail weave she could find, staring at the patterns until she could see how they wove together. Anne's 16-year journey in metals has taken her from an in-depth exploration of ancient chain mail patterns to a study of traditional metalsmith techniques and currently, to fine-silver metalworking.

Double-Cross Link
bracelet

During a trip to the silver markets of Taxco, Mexico, the region that supplied silver to the Spanish court in the 1500s and is a living monument to the art of working with silver, a double-cross link chain created by a local artist caught my eye. This design is popular with novices because it produces a polished look and presents satisfying challenges.

a

b

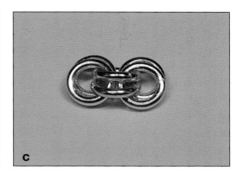

c

d

e

f

g

h

i

In these photographs, the rings that join the sections of jump rings are black to help you see them more clearly.

[1] Assemble 2+2+2 links: Prepare to assemble the bracelet links by closing 84 and opening 42 jump rings.

[2] Scoop up four closed rings on one open ring **(a)** and close the open ring.

[3] Repeat the path with a second open ring **(b)** for a strand of three sets of links with two rings in each section. This is called a 2+2+2 link **(c)**. Assemble 21 2+2+2 link sections for a 7-in. (18cm) bracelet.

[4] Join the sections: Open 40 rings. These will be used to join the 2+2+2 link sections. Position two 2+2+2 link sections with one centered above the other to form a T-shape **(d)**.

[5] To help describe the next step, I will call the cross section at the top of the T "Part A" and the vertical section below it "Part B." Attach these two sections, using the newly opened jump rings. First, connect the top rings of Part B to one of the side rings of Part A. Connect the same top rings of Part B to the other set of side rings on Part A **(e, f)**.

[6] Place another 2+2+2 link at a 90-degree angle at the base of the section you just finished assembling. Use two open rings to attach this link in the same fashion **(g)**.

[7] Continue connecting the 2+2+2 link sections in this manner until you reach the desired length for your bracelet **(h)**.

[8] Attach the clasp: Use jump rings to connect the final links at either end of your bracelet to the clasp pieces. If using a lobster claw clasp instead of

the toggle clasp shown, add a jump ring on the opposite end to act as the loop. Be sure to end the pattern so the chain can lie flat **(i)**.

materials

bracelet 8 in. (20 cm)
- **170** (approx.) sterling silver 3.0mm ID 18-gauge jump rings
- Sterling silver toggle or lobster claw clasp

tools
- Bentnose pliers
- Chainnose pliers

Jump rings for all of Anne's projects are available from annemitchell.net

Chain Mail Overlay bracelet

Layered jump rings provide depth and form intriguing shapes in this bracelet. A basic 2+2 chain forms the foundation of this chain, but you'll layer jump rings to create the visual depth that takes this piece from straightforward to smashing. Although the bracelet looks intricate, the steps are easy to follow because you'll add one ring at a time.

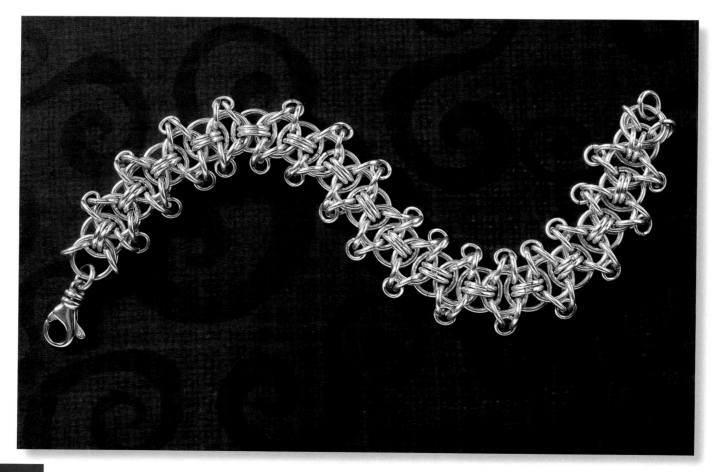

a

b

c

d

e

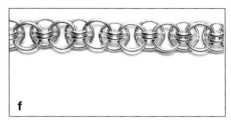

f

g

h

i

j

k

materials

bracelet 8 in. (20cm)
- Sterling silver jump rings
  - 50 16-gauge, 7.5mm ID
  - 98 16-gauge, 5.0mm ID
  - 30 18-gauge, 3.0mm ID
- Clasp

tools
- Chainnose pliers
- Bentnose pliers

[1] Close 34 7.5mm jump rings and open 32 5mm jump rings. Thread four 7.5mm rings on one 5mm ring **(a)**, and close the ring. Thread a second 5mm ring through the same four 7.5mm rings **(b)**.

[2] Thread a 5mm ring through two of the 7.5mm rings, and add two more 7.5mm rings **(c)**. Close the ring. Thread a second 5mm ring through those same four 7.5mm rings, and close the ring **(d)**.

[3] Repeat step 2 until the chain is the desired length. For an 8-in. (20cm) bracelet, use all of the rings indicated in step 1.

[4] Open 16 7.5mm rings. Starting at one end of the chain, loop a 7.5mm ring around the end two 5mm rings,

positioning it between the two layers of 7.5mm rings **(e)**. Close the ring. Repeat along the length of the chain **(f)**.

[5] Open 64 5mm rings. Thread a 5mm ring through the opening created by the overlap of the three layered 7.5mm rings **(g)**, and close the ring. Repeat along this edge of the chain, then repeat along the opposite edge **(h)**.

[6] Open 30 3mm rings. Starting on one end of the chain and skipping the first 5mm ring, thread a 3mm ring through the second and third 5mm rings **(i)**. Close the ring. Continue connecting pairs of rings, skipping the last 5mm ring. Repeat along the opposite edge of the chain, skipping the first and last rings.

[7] Open a 5mm ring, and thread it through the first pair of 7.5mm rings on one end of the chain and through one half of a clasp **(j)**. Close the ring.

[8] Open a second 5mm ring, thread it through the pair of 7.5mm rings on the other end of the chain, and close the ring **(k)**.

Beyond Chain
bracelet & necklace

Combine two classic chain mail techniques—Japanese Overlay and Corduroy Weave—to make an unusual chain with layers and a flat base. Add color to the chain with crystals, as shown here, or substitute glass beads, semiprecious stones, or freshwater pearls.

materials

bracelet 8 in. (20cm)
- **23** (approx.) sterling silver jump rings, 10.0mm ID, 15-gauge wire
- **86** (approx.) sterling silver jump rings, 5.5mm ID, 17-gauge wire
- **11** 6mm round crystals
- Lobster claw clasp
- **2** crimp beads
- Flexible beading wire, .014

choker 14 in. (36cm)
- **63** (approx.) sterling silver jump rings, 10.0mm ID, 15-gauge wire
- **172** (approx.) sterling silver jump rings, 5.5mm ID, 17-gauge wire
- **22** 6mm round crystals
- Lobster claw clasp
- **2** crimp beads
- Flexible beading wire, .014

tools
- Chainnose pliers
- Bentnose pliers
- Crimping pliers
- Wire cutters

a

b

c

d

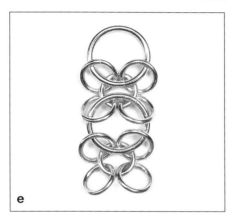

e

Bracelet

[1] Connect the jump rings: Close 44 and open 11 5.5mm jump rings.

[2] Slide four closed 5.5mm rings on an open 5.5mm ring **(a).** Close the ring. Repeat with the remaining rings to make 11 four-in-one sets.

[3] Open 12 10mm rings.

[4] Separate the four rings in a four-in-one set into two pairs. Flip one pair of rings so they are side by side on your work surface **(b)**. Slide a 10mm ring through the two side-by-side 5.5mm rings **(c)**.

[5] Close the 10mm ring, and tape it to your work surface so the rings are easier to position. Flip the other pair of 5.5mm rings toward each other. The inside edge of the rings will touch, and the rings will not lie flat **(d)**.

[6] Repeat step 4. Connect the new 10mm ring to the available pair of 5.5mm rings on the previous four-in-one set. Remove the tape, close the 10mm ring, and flip the next pair of 5.5mm rings as in step 5 **(e)**.

f

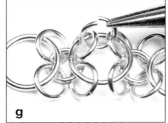

g

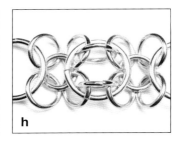

h

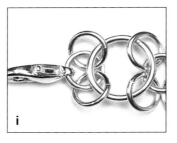

i

j

k

[7] Continue connecting four-in-one sets with the remaining 10mm rings from step 3 **(f).** You won't need to secure the chain to your work surface. Connect the last 10mm ring to the end pair of 5.5mm rings.

[8] Open 20 5.5mm rings.

[9] Starting at the second 10mm ring on the chain, slide a 5.5mm ring through the top two 5.5mm rings within the 10mm ring **(g).** Close the 5.5mm ring, and repeat with the bottom two 5.5mm rings **(h).** Continue along the length of the chain.

[10] Close one 5.5mm ring, and open 10 5.5mm rings.

[11] Working on one end of the chain, connect two 5.5mm rings to the end 10mm ring. Flip the rings as shown, and connect the lobster claw clasp to

the two 5.5mm rings using a third ring **(i).** Connect two rings to the 5.5mm rings within the end 10mm ring, as in step 9 **(j).**

[12] Repeat step 11 at the other end of the chain, substituting the closed 5.5mm ring for the lobster claw clasp.

[13] Open 11 10mm rings.

[14] Starting at one end, slide a 10mm ring through the vertical 5.5mm rings in the centers of the first two 10mm rings **(k).** Close the ring. Repeat along the chain **(l). Photo m** shows the side view of the finished chain.

Color pop
Crystals nestled within a sterling silver bracelet and choker add a lively burst of color.

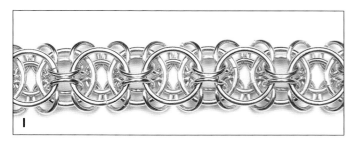

l

m

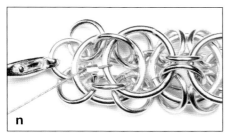

n

o

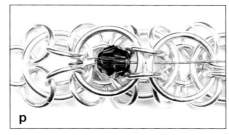

p

[15] String the crystals: Cut a 1-ft. (30cm) length of flexible beading wire, and string a crimp bead. Starting at one end of the chain, slide the end of the wire between the two vertical 5.5mm rings and up through the center of the 10mm ring. Bring the wire back through the crimp bead. Position the crimp bead next to the 10mm ring, crimp the crimp bead (Basics), and trim the wire tail as close to the crimp bead as possible **(n)**.

[16] String a crystal, and bring the end of the wire under the other side of the 10mm ring, between the next two vertical 5.5mm rings, and out through the center of the next 10mm ring **(o)**.

[17] Pull on the wire, popping the crystal into the center of the first 10mm ring **(p)**.

[18] Repeat steps 16 and 17 along the chain. String a crimp bead after the last crystal, and crimp the wire to the other end as in step 15.

Choker

Follow the directions for the bracelet, using the number of jump rings necessary to reach your desired length. When stringing the crystals, use a length of flexible beading wire 4 in. (10cm) longer than the chain length.

Technique Tip

To keep the crystals from sliding inside the chain and to hide the beading wire between the crystals, adapt the instructions as follows: Work steps 15–17. String a 2mm round silver bead, a 4mm crystal, and a 2mm bead. Position the crystal under the two 5.5mm rings. Repeat this pattern, ending with a crimp bead instead of a 2mm bead. The photos below show the crystals' placement on the top, side, and bottom of the chain.

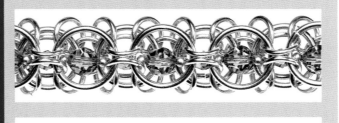

Ancient Links
necklace

Blending Byzantine and Queen's Link chain-making techniques results in a simple yet stunning necklace. The patterns are remarkably similar, so combining them in one piece is a natural evolution. Though the instructions alternate the Byzantine and Queen's Link, you can make a bracelet or necklace in either of the patterns or change the lengths of the sequences as desired.

a

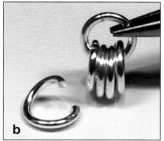

b

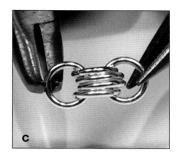

c

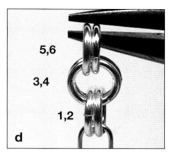

5,6

3,4

1,2

d

5

6

e

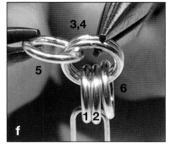

3,4

5

6

1 2

f

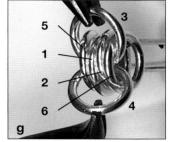

5

1

2

6

3

4

g

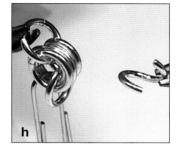

h

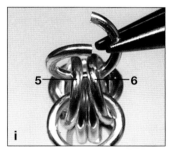

5

6

i

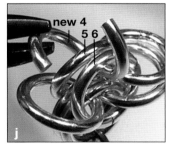

new 4

5 6

j

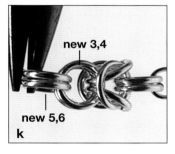

new 3,4

new 5,6

k

Begin the necklace

[1] Use the large (5.5mm) jump rings for this section of the necklace. Close four and open two rings **(a)**.

[2] Slide the four closed rings onto one open ring. Close the open ring **(b)**.

[3] Repeat step 2 with the remaining open ring **(c)**.

[4] Bring the two rings closed in steps 2 and 3 together, then separate the four rings strung in step 2 into two sets of two. This strand of three sets of two links each will be called a 2+2+2. Link a paper clip on one end of the strand to weight and stabilize the strand it, making the chain easier to construct. (This will also make it easier to find the beginning of the

necklace when—not if!—you accidentally drop it.) Mentally number the rings in the following order: The rings with the paper clip are 1 and 2; the middle rings are 3 and 4; and the top rings are 5 and 6 **(d)**.

Create the Queen's Link sequence

[5] Open 32 large jump rings. Grasp rings 5 and 6 with the bentnose pliers in your recessive hand; curve the tips of the pliers toward your work. With chainnose pliers in your dominant hand, flip one of the 5/6 rings out from the jaws of the bentnose pliers **(e)** and let it fall to one side.

[6] Grasp rings 3 and 4 with the chainnose pliers **(f)**. Let the remaining 5/6 ring fall to the opposite side.

[7] With the bentnose pliers in your recessive hand and the chainnose pliers in your dominant hand, grasp rings 3 and 4, one ring in each plier, and spread them apart so you can see all four remaining rings lined up between rings 3 and 4. The order of the rings is 5, 1, 2, 6 **(g)**.

[8] Drop the ring held with your dominant hand and hold one ring in the bentnose pliers with your recessive hand. Using the chainnose pliers in your dominant hand, pick up one open ring **(h)**.

[9] Scoop up rings 5 and 6 with this new ring **(i)**. Be careful not to include rings 1 and 2 in the open ring. Drop the ring held

materials

necklace 18½–19 in.
(47.0–48.3cm)

- **350** (approx.) 5.5mm ID 16-gauge sterling silver jump rings
- **130** (approx.) 4.0mm ID 16-gauge sterling silver jump rings
- Sterling silver lobster claw clasp

tools

- Chainnose pliers
- Bentnose pliers
- Paper clip
- Ruler

with the bentnose pliers. Close the new jump ring.

[10] Repeat step 9 using another open jump ring. These rings will be the new 3 and 4 **(j)**.

[11] Hold the new rings 3 and 4 in your recessive hand using the bentnose pliers. Add two new jump rings onto 3 and 4. These rings **(k)** will be your new 5 and 6. This completes one Queen's Link sequence.

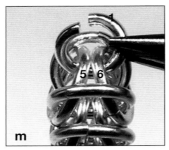
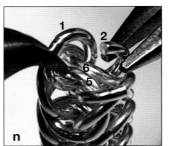
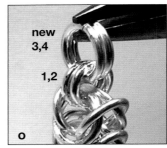

m

n

o

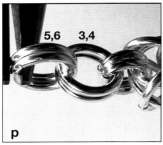

p

[12] Repeat the Queen's Link sequence for approximately 1½ in. (3.8cm) or until you've used all 32 opened rings **(l)**. End the sequence holding a new 5 and 6. (If you want to make a necklace entirely of the Queen's Link, simply continue until you reach the desired length and then proceed to "Add closure," below.)

Create the Byzantine sequence

[13] Open 10 4mm rings and 16 large 5.5mm rings.

Grasp rings 5 and 6 (from the end of the Queen's Link sequence) with the bentnose pliers in your recessive hand, having the tips of the pliers curved toward your work. Using the chainnose pliers in your dominant hand, flip one of the 5/6 rings out from the jaws of the bentnose pliers and let it fall to one side, as in step 5. Grasp rings 3 and 4 with the chainnose pliers. Let go of the remaining 5/6 ring and let it fall to the opposite side, as in step 6.

With the bentnose pliers in your recessive hand and the chainnose pliers in your dominant hand, grip rings 3 and 4, one ring in each plier, and spread them apart so that they are off to each side and you can see all four remaining rings lined up between rings 3 and 4, as in step 7. The order of the rings is 5, 1, 2, 6.

[14] Drop the ring held with your dominant hand. Continue holding one ring in the bentnose pliers with your recessive hand. Using the chainnose pliers in your dominant hand, pick up a small open jump ring. Place the small ring through rings 5 and 6 **(m)**. Be careful not to scoop up rings 1 and 2. Drop the ring held with the bentnose pliers and close this new jump ring using both pliers.

[15] Repeat step 13 using another open small jump ring. These rings are the new 1 and 2 **(n)**.

[16] Hold the new rings 1 and 2 in your recessive hand using the bentnose pliers. Add two large jump rings onto 1 and 2. These two new rings will be your new 3 and 4 **(o)**.

[17] Add two more large jump rings onto 3 and 4. These two new jump rings will be 5 and 6 **(p)**. You have completed one Byzantine sequence.

[18] Repeat the entire Byzantine sequence until you have used 10 small rings and 16 large rings **(q)**.

[19] Alternate the Queen's Link and the Byzantine sequences until you reach the desired length for your piece. Each subsequent Queen's Link sequence requires 36 large rings to be opened, and the

Byzantine sequence requires 10 small and 16 large rings to be opened. Open only the required number of rings for each sequence as you work; this will keep your section lengths even and your work surface tidy so you won't get confused.

Add closure

[20] Scoop up the last two large rings with a small ring. Loop the small ring through the clasp and close the ring. Loop another small ring through the two rings joined with a paper clip. Close the ring and remove the paper clip.

John Fetvedt

"Chain making combines art, mathematics, and construction."

John works in chain making, metal forming, casting, forging, and stone setting, among other areas. Chain making is of particular interest to him as each pattern combines art, in the way the finished jewelry decorates the body; mathematics, in calculating the ring size to use when changing the gauge or pattern; and construction techniques, like solving a jigsaw puzzle. John's mentors include Mary Ann Scherr, Blaine Lewis, Charles Lewton-Brain, Cynthia Eid, Thomas Mann, and Betty Helen Longhi.

Half-Byzantine
hoop earrings

Funky, swinging hoop earrings have cycled in and out of fashion for as long as people have been wearing jewelry. This new take on the trend moves toward a more subtle style, with three larger hoops linked in a tapered shape by half of a Byzantine chain pattern. It's the gauge of the larger jump rings that allows them to fit inside the connecting rings, so if you want a bolder look, you can increase the diameters of the larger rings as much as you wish as long as you keep their gauge the same.

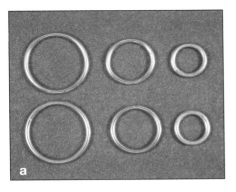

a

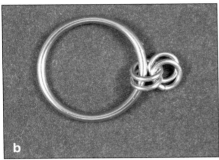

b

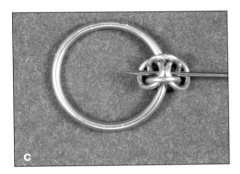

c

materials

earrings 2½ in. (64mm)

- Sterling silver jump rings
  - **32** 20-gauge (0.8mm), 3mm ID
  - **2** 16-gauge (1.3mm), 6.5mm ID
  - **2** 16-gauge (1.3mm), 9.5mm ID
  - **2** 16-gauge (1.3mm), 13mm ID
- Pair of earring wires

Kits for all of John's projects are available at bijoux-de-terre.com

tools & supplies

- **2** pairs of chainnose, bentnose, or flatnose pliers
- Needle tool or pick
- Torch station (optional): torch, paste solder (medium), soldering pad or firebrick, pickle pot with pickle, quench bowl, copper tongs, pick
- Tumbler, steel shot, burnishing compound (optional)

[1] Close two 6.5mm jump rings, two 9.5mm jump rings, and two 13mm jump rings **(a)**. To give your earrings a more finished look, permanently close the cuts in these jump rings by fusing or soldering them. (See "Fuse or Solder?" right.)

[2] Thread a 3mm ring onto a 13mm ring and close it; repeat with another 3mm ring. Thread a 3mm ring through the first pair of 3mm rings and close it; repeat with a second 3mm ring **(b)**.

[3] Flip the second pair of 3mm rings back, one to each side of the first pair. Insert a needle tool or pick above the 13mm ring to hold the first pair of rings apart and expose the second pair **(c)**.

Fuse or Solder?

You don't need a complex torch setup to fuse or solder jump rings—a handheld butane torch and a soldering surface will do. Relatively inexpensive butane torches are available at most hardware stores.

If your jump rings are made of Argentium sterling silver or fine silver, you can either fuse or solder them. (I find that fusing the rings results in a smoother seam.) If your jump rings are made of sterling silver or gold, they can only be soldered.

To fuse your jump rings, first close them, making sure that the ends are aligned and tightly abutting each other. Lay the rings on a soldering pad or firebrick with the cuts facing toward you.

Working on one ring at a time, gently heat the whole ring by moving your torch in a circular motion, then concentrate the point of the flame on the cut. When the area on either side of the cut turns cloudy, the metal is almost hot enough to fuse, so get ready to move the torch away. As soon as the metal at the join becomes shiny and the join appears somewhat less defined, remove the torch.

The join may not disappear completely, but the ring will be fused. If you're using Argentium sterling, let the rings cool a bit before you quench them; Argentium sterling is somewhat fragile when it's hot.

To solder jump rings, first close them, and make sure the ends are aligned and tightly abutting each other. Lay the rings on a soldering pad or firebrick, with the cuts facing away from you. Dab a small amount of paste solder to the inside of each cut. Turn the board or brick so the cuts are facing you.

Working on one ring at a time, gently heat the whole ring; then concentrate the tip of the flame on the cut. The solder will melt and move toward the heat of the torch. Remove the torch as soon as the solder has flowed into the join. Quench, pickle, and rinse.

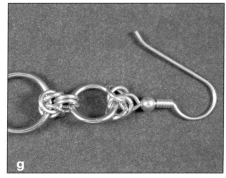

[4] Insert a 3mm ring alongside the needle tool. Slide a 9.5mm ring onto the 3mm ring, and close the 3mm ring. Remove the needle tool, and thread and close a second 3mm ring alongside the first one **(d)**.

[5] Thread two 3mm rings onto the 9.5mm ring and close them. Thread two more 3mm rings through the previous pair and close them. Flip the second pair of rings back, one to each side of the first pair. Insert the needle tool above the 9.5mm ring to hold the first pair apart and expose the second pair **(e)**.

[6] Insert a 3mm ring alongside the needle tool. Slide a 6.5mm ring onto the 3mm ring, and close the 3mm ring. Remove the needle tool, and thread and close a second 3mm ring alongside the first one **(f)**.

[7] Thread two 3mm rings onto the 6.5mm ring and close them. Thread two more 3mm rings through the previous pair and close them. Flip the second pair of rings back, one to each side of the first pair. Insert the needle tool to

hold the first pair apart and expose the second pair. Open the loop of an earring wire and insert the loop alongside the needle tool. Close the loop and remove the needle tool **(g)**.

[8] Repeat to make a matching earring. It is important that you start each earring with the 13mm rings so that the direction of the Byzantine pattern will be the same on both earrings. Burnish your earrings in a tumbler with steel shot and burnishing compound, if desired.

Mixed metals
For variety,
try combining silver
and gold-filled rings.

Mixed-Metal Double-Barrel bracelet

Barrel chain is an elementary chain mail pattern that uses just one jump ring size in a straightforward weave. But you can use the same simple pattern to make a complex-looking chain. Because barrel chain has a naturally diagonal orientation when it's worn, two barrel chains side by side will nest together, forming a dense pattern with a lovely, fluid drape. To make the look even richer, you can mix and match anodized niobium jump rings within the weave.

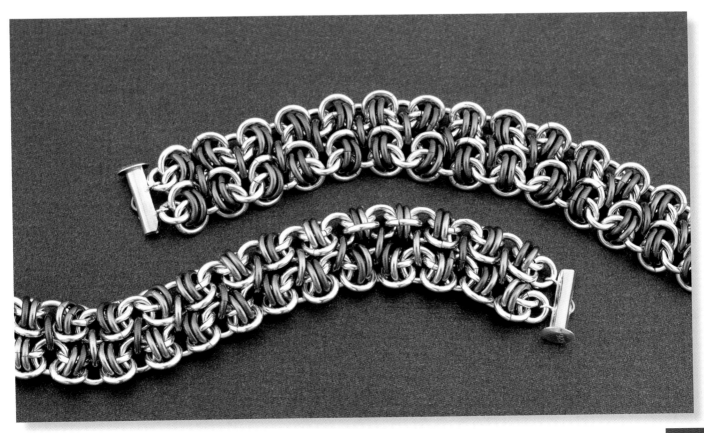

a

b

c

[1] Place a two-strand clasp on your work surface. Using two pairs of pliers, open two 3.2mm jump rings , and attach one to each loop on one side of the clasp **(a)**.

[2] Using one of the 3.2mm rings as the first ring in a chain, make the first

link of a barrel chain (see "Basic Barrel Chain," below) using 4.4mm Argentium and niobium rings **(b)**.

[3] Starting with the second 3.2mm ring on the clasp, make the first link of a second barrel chain **(c)**.

In my bracelet, all the horizontal jump rings are Argentium, and all the vertical jump rings are niobium. You can, of course, create this pattern using all one metal, or mix and match metals.

Basic Barrel Chain

This chain is also known as a "Double Vision Chain," and uses jump rings with an aspect ratio of 3.4.

Thread scrap wire, a twist tie, or a paper clip through one closed jump ring (green in the example below). Thread a second ring (blue) through the

first ring, and close it. Then thread a third ring (red) through the second, and close it. Repeat to thread a fourth ring (red) through the second ring (blue) **(a)**.

Here's the path **(b)** for the next ring: Thread a fifth ring up through the back of the paired

rings at the end of the chain and then through the back of the first ring on the chain. This action pushes the red rings upward into their horizontal position to make the barrel **(c)**.

NOTE: If it's more comfortable for you to thread your fifth ring through the front of the paired rings, be sure to thread it through the front of the first ring, and close it at the back of the pattern. Whichever threading direction you choose, be sure to maintain that same direction for the whole length of the chain.

Close a sixth ring through both of the rings at the working end of the chain **(d)**. This completes one barrel link. The last ring of this link will act as the first ring of the next link **(e)**.

For this project, I used niobium jump rings in place of the red rings in the basic barrel chain tutorial, and Argentium jump rings in place of the blue and green rings.

a

b

c

d

e

d

e

f

g

[4] Attach a second barrel link to each of the two chains **(d)**.

[5] Thread a 4.4mm niobium ring through the single ring that connects the first and second barrel links of each chain, and close it **(e)**.

[6] Add a third barrel link to each of the two chains, and use a niobium jump ring to connect the single Argentium ring between the second and third barrel links of each chain **(f)**.

[7] Continue adding barrel links to each of the two chains, connecting the two chains after adding each new pair of barrel links, until the bracelet is the desired length. Use the remaining two 3.2mm Argentium rings to connect the end of each chain to the clasp **(g)**.

Tumble-polish the bracelet for 20 minutes (See "Burnishing Chains," right).

materials

bracelet 7½ in. (19.1cm)

- Argentium sterling silver jump rings:
  - **148** 16-gauge (1.3mm), 4.4mm ID
  - **4** 16-gauge (1.3mm), 3.2mm ID
- Niobium jump rings:
  - **124** 16-gauge (1.3mm), 4.4mm ID
- Sterling silver 2-strand clasp

tools

- **2** pairs of chainnose, bentnose, or flatnose pliers
- Needle tool or pick

Burnishing Chains

SAFETY NOTE: Never attempt to use a polishing wheel or any powered rotary device to polish chains. Chains can cause serious injury if they catch in a high-powered wheel.

The best way to polish a chain is to burnish it in a small tumbler with stainless steel shot and a burnishing liquid. I have found that 30 minutes of tumbling is usually adequate. When I'm working with niobium jump rings, I shorten that time to 20 minutes to avoid damaging the niobium's vivid colors.

I use a Lortone Model 3-1.5B tumbler in my studio, and I use a tumbler from Harbor Freight in my classes and workshops. I use a barrel from the Lortone tumbler (it's a little smaller than the Harbor Freight barrel) in both tumblers, and 2 lb. (0.907 kg) of stainless steel mixed shot with Super Sunsheen Burnishing Compound. (Make sure you get stainless steel shot, or you'll spend all of your time trying to keep your shot clean.) Since I use my tumbler nearly every day, I leave the used shot in the barrel, covered with the burnishing compound, until I'm ready to use the tumbler again. Then, I rinse the barrel and shot in water and use fresh burnishing compound for its next use.

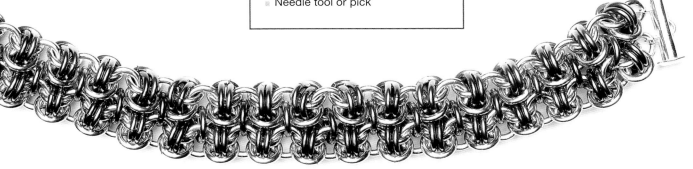

Double-Cross
Chain set

Pair tiny silver and niobium rings to make a dainty jewelry set.

materials

anklet 9½ in. (24.1cm);
bracelet 7¾ in. (19.7cm)
earrings

- Sterling silver jump rings:
  - 20-gauge (0.81mm), 3/32 in. ID (A rings): **232** for anklet, **184** for bracelet, **32** for earrings
  - 18-gauge (1.02mm), 1/8 in. ID: **1** for anklet or bracelet
  - 18-gauge (1.02mm), 3/32 in. ID: **1** for anklet or bracelet
  - Niobium jumpbrings (B rings): 20-gauge (0.81mm), 3/32 in. ID: **78** for anklet, **62** for bracelet, **12** for earrings
- Lobster claw clasp for anklet or bracelet
- Pair of earring wires

tools

- **2** pairs of chainnose, bentnose, or flatnose pliers
- Needle tool or pick

a

c

e

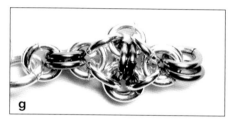

g

b

d

f

h

i

j

Anklet or bracelet

[1] To make an anklet, open 232 3/32-in. sterling silver jump rings (A rings) and close 78 3/32-in. niobium jump rings (B rings). To make a bracelet, open 184 A rings and close 62 3/32-in. niobium jump rings (B rings). For either piece, close a 1/8-in sterling silver jump ring, and attach a scrap piece of beading wire to it **(a)**.

[2] Build a 2+2+2 chain, using two As, two Bs, and two As **(b)**.

[3] Attach an A to the end pair of As. Add an A to double it **(c)** it.

[4] Separate the pair of As just added, and attach an A and a pair of Bs to one of them. Double the A **(d)**.

[5] Slide an A through the remaining A from step 3 and the pair of Bs added in step 4. Double the new A **(e)**.

[6] Attach an A to each end pair of As **(f)**.

[7] Attach an A and two Bs to the As added in step 6. Double the new A **(g)**.

[8] Attach an A to the end pair of Bs. Double the A. Repeat steps 3–8 until the chain is the desired length **(h)**.

[9] Open a 3/32-in. 18-gauge ring, attach it to the end pair of As and a clasp, and close the ring **(i)**. If desired, tumble-polish the chain in a tumbler with stainless steel shot and burnishing compound.

Earrings

Open 32 3/32-in. sterling silver jump rings (A rings) and close 12 3/32-in. niobium jump rings (B rings). Follow steps 2–8. Open the loop of an earring wire, attach an end pair of As, and close the loop **(j)**. Make a second earring.

Note: "Double" simply means follow the same path with a second, same-size ring.

Graceful Chain
earrings

To create supple, tapered earrings that drape like fabric, you'll weave fine-gauge jump rings in this European 4-in-1 pattern. You can change the length of the earrings by adding or removing five-ring rows. For an alternate look, try adding a top-drilled bead on the bottom jump ring.

a

b

c

d

e

f

g

h

i

To make it easier for you to understand the pattern, the photos show colored jump rings that are larger than the size you'll actually use. For the actual earrings, you'll likely want to use jump rings in all one color.

[1] Open 138 or 188 jump rings and close the remaining two. (For a pair of 1½-in./3.8cm earrings, you'll use 140 rings. For 2-in./5cm earrings, you'll use 190 rings.) Set aside one closed ring and half of the open rings for the second earring (see note, page 50).

[2] String a closed (blue) jump ring on a scrap piece of wire or paper clip; you can hold onto this as you work.

[3] Close two (red) rings around the first (blue) ring **(a)**.

[4] Working the third row of rings from left to right, thread a (blue) ring through the first (red) ring on the left **(b)** and close the (blue) ring.

Thread a (blue) ring through the first and second (red) rings **(c)**, and close

the ring. The new ring should overlap the (blue) ring previously added.

Thread a (blue) ring through just the second (red) ring **(d)**, and close it. The new ring should overlap the previously added ring.

[5] Working the fourth row of rings from right to left, thread a (red) ring through the first (blue) ring **(e)**, and close the ring.

Thread a (red) ring through the first and second (blue) rings **(f)**, making sure this new (red) ring overlaps the first ring in this row. Close the ring.

Thread a (red) ring through the second and third (blue) rings **(g)**, making sure the new (red) ring is overlapping the others. Close the ring.

Thread a (red) ring through the third (blue) ring **(h)**, and close the ring.

[6] Work the fifth row of five rings from left to right, repeating the established

materials

earrings

1½ in. (3.8cm) or 2 in. (5cm)

- **140 or 190** 22-gauge jump rings, 2.4mm inside diameter
- **2** top-drilled beads (optional)
- Pair of earring wires

tools& supplies

- **2** pairs of chainnose, bentnose, or flatnose pliers
- Tumbler, stainless steel shot, and burnishing compound

pattern: Go through the first (red) ring with the first (blue) ring. Go through the first and second (red) ring with the second (blue) ring. Go through the second and third (red) ring with the third (blue) ring. Go through the third and fourth (red) ring with the fourth (blue) ring. Go through the fourth (red) ring with the fifth (blue) ring **(i)**.

j

k

l

m

n

o

[7] Working right to left, add another row of five rings: Go through the first (blue) ring with the first (red) ring. Go through the first and second (blue) rings with the second (red) ring. Go through the second and third (blue) rings with the third (red) ring. Go through the third and fourth (blue) rings with the fourth (red) ring. Go through the fourth and fifth (blue) rings with the fifth (red) ring **(j)**.

At this point in the pattern, you are no longer lengthening the rows, so, unlike previous rows, you don't close a ring around the single last ring in the row.

[8] Repeat step 7 to add five-ring rows, working back and forth. For the shorter earrings, work a total of 10 five-ring rows. For the longer earrings, work 15 five-ring rows.

[9] After the desired number of five-ring rows are in place, you'll want to decrease the ring count for each row. To do this, don't thread any rings through a single jump ring in the previous row; just connect pairs of rings in the previous row. For the four-ring row, close new rings through the first and second rings, second and third rings, third and fourth rings, and fourth and fifth rings **(k)**.

[10] For the three-ring row, close new rings through the first and second rings, second and third rings, and third and fourth rings **(l)**.

[11] For the two-ring row, close new rings through the first and second rings, and second and third rings **(m)**.

[12] For the single-ring row **(n)**, thread a top-drilled bead on the ring, if desired, and close the ring around the two rings in the previous row, making sure the ring lies correctly.

[13] Remove the wire or paper clip from the first jump ring. Open the loop of an earring wire, attach the top ring of the earring, and close the loop.

[14] Make a second earring in the mirror image of the first by working step 4 from right to left. Position the rings so they overlap as shown **(o)**. Remember that the new row always starts with the last ring added to the previous row.

[15] To polish the earrings, put them in a tumbler with steel shot and burnishing compound for two hours.

Technique Tip

Try this technique to keep track of all the jump rings:
• Separate the rings into piles. Make a pile of 10 rings for the first four rows and 10 rings for the last four. Put the remaining rings in five-ring piles.

Vanessa Walilko

"I love chain mail because of the rhythmic process involved with its creation."

A designer of chain mail jewelry and wearable art, Vanessa continually seeks ways to push the boundaries of the art form. Her work explores the interplay of fashion and armor, and how we construct our identity through what we wear. Her chain mail fashion designs have won international awards and have been featured in exhibitions throughout North America, Australia, and England.

Art Deco
necklace

The clean, elegant lines of graduated box chain pair with geometric details to celebrate the art and architecture of a bygone era.

a

b

c

d

e

f

g

h

materials

necklace 17 in. (43.2cm)

- Sterling silver, copper, or gold-filled jump rings:
  - **6** ¼-in. ID, 18-gauge (1.02mm) (ring A)
  - **18** ¼-in. ID, 16-gauge (1.29mm) (ring B)
  - **12** ⁹/₃₂-in. ID, 16-gauge (1.29mm) (ring C)
  - **48** ⁷/₃₂-in. ID, 17-gauge (1.15mm) (ring D)
  - **48** ¹¹/₆₄-in. ID, 19-gauge (0.91mm) (ring E)
  - **48** ⁹/₆₄-in. ID, 20-gauge (0.81mm) (ring F)
  - **24** ⅛-in. ID, 21-gauge (0.72mm) (ring G)
  - **4** ⁵/₃₂ in. ID, 18-gauge (1.02mm) (ring H)
  - **1** ⁷/₃₂-in. ID, 14-gauge (1.63mm) (ring I)
- 10 in. (25.4cm) sterling rope chain
- figure-8 clasp
- **3** 20mm Swarovski Elements Cosmic Rings
- **3** 20mm Swarovski Elements Triangles

tools

- **2** pairs of chainnose, bentnose, or flatnose pliers

Kits for Vanessa's projects are available at kalibutterfly.com.

Crystal units

[1] Before you begin, refer to the materials list and open all of the A, B, and H jump rings. Open six C rings and open 24 D, F, and G rings. Close the remaining jump rings. Slide an open A ring through one side of a crystal triangle, and close it. Repeat with a second A ring **(a)**.

[2] Pick up two closed C rings with an open C ring, and slide the open ring onto the triangle in between the two A rings. Close the ring. Slide a second open C ring through the triangle and the two closed C rings. Close the ring **(b)**.

[3] Let the two hanging C rings fall to either side of the triangle. With your fingers, pinch the hanging rings together and squeeze them up so that the two C rings above them part into a V **(c)**. The space between the V is where you add new rings. You have created your first unit of box chain.

[4] Slide an open D ring through two closed D rings and then through the two C rings between the V. Close the D ring. Slide a second open D ring along the same path, and close it **(d)**.

[5] Repeat steps 3 and 4 with the following sets of ring sizes: E, F, G, F, E, D **(e)**.

[6] Let the hanging D rings fall to either side of the chain, and push them toward the center. Slide an open B ring through the two D rings between the V and then through a crystal ring. Close the B ring. Slide a second B ring along the same path, and close it **(f)**.

[7] Repeat steps 1–6 twice to create a total of three crystal units **(g)**.

Connect the crystal units

[8] Slide an open B ring through a crystal ring, and close it. Repeat to add a second B ring to the crystal ring **(h)**.

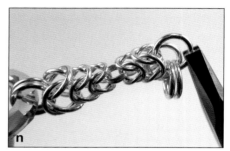

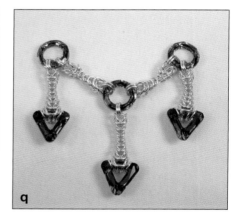

[9] Slide an open D ring through two closed D rings and then through the two B rings. Close the D ring. Slide a second open D ring along the same path, and close it **(i)**.

[10] Let the D rings at the end of the chain fall to either side of the chain. Squeeze them toward the center until the rings part into a V. Pick up two closed E rings with an open E ring, then slide the open ring through the D rings between the V. Close the open ring. Slide a second open E ring along the same path, and close it **(j)**.

[11] Let the E rings at the end of the chain fall to either side of the chain. Squeeze the E rings toward the center until they part into a V. Slide an open F ring through two closed F rings and then through the E rings between the V. Close the open ring. Slide a second open F ring along the same path, and close it **(k)**.

[12] Let the F rings at the end of the chain fall to either side of the chain. Squeeze them toward the center until they part into a V. Slide an open G ring through the F rings between the V, and close it. Repeat to add a second G ring along the same path **(l)**.

[13] Slide an open F ring through two closed F rings and the two G rings. Close the open ring. Repeat to add a second F ring along the same path **(m)**.

[14] Let the F rings at the end of the chain fall to either side of the chain. Squeeze them toward the center until they part into a V. Slide an open E ring through two closed E rings and then through the F rings between the V. Close the open ring. Repeat to add a second E ring along the same path **(n)**.

[15] Repeat step 14 with D rings **(o)**.

[16] Let the D rings fall to either side of the chain and squeeze them toward the center. Slide an open B ring through the D rings between the V. Slide the crystal ring of the second crystal unit through the open ring, then close the ring. Repeat to add a second B ring along the same path **(p)**.

[17] Repeat steps 8–16 to connect the third crystal unit to the piece **(q)**.

[18] Slide an open B ring through the crystal ring on the left side. Close the ring. Repeat to add a second B ring to the crystal ring (r).

[19] Use the two B rings as the start of another box weave. Add four units of box weave in the following sizes: D, E, F, and G (s).

[20] Slide an open H ring through the G rings between the V and then through the last two links of a 5-in. (12.7cm) rope chain. Close the ring (t).

[21] Slide an open H ring through the last two links of the open end of the rope chain, then through a figure-8 clasp. Close the ring (u).

[22] Repeat steps 18–20 to add the box chain weave and a second rope chain to the crystal ring on the right side (v).

[23] Slide an open H ring through the last two links of the open end of rope chain, then through the closed I ring. Close the H ring (w).

Reversible
Chain Reaction
bracelet

Begin with a basic European 4-in-1 chain, add half-Persian edging, and connect the edges to create a double-sided bracelet of interlocking chain mail weaves.

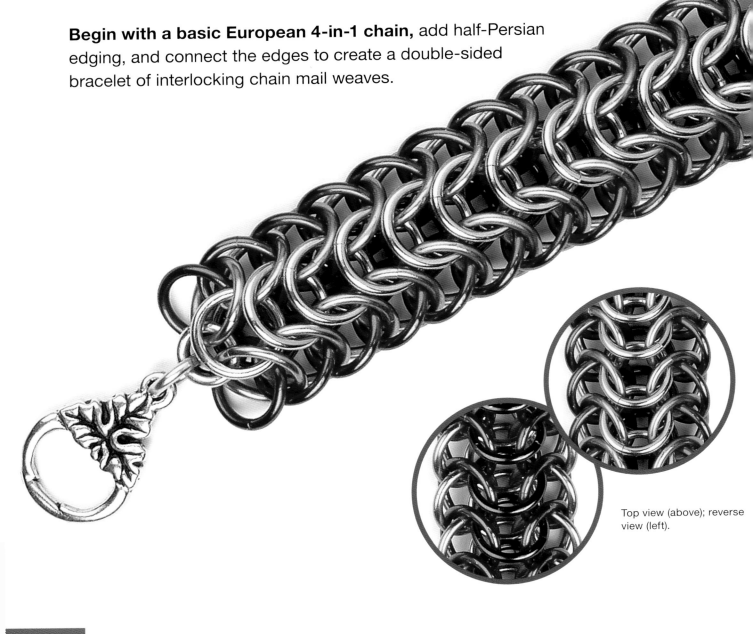

Top view (above); reverse view (left).

materials
warm-tone bracelet
7 in. (18cm)

- 6mm anodized aluminum jump rings, 18-gauge:
  - **62** color A (orange)
  - **62** color B (red)
  - **30** color C (gold)
  - **30** color D (brown)
- 3.9mm ID anodized aluminum jump rings, 18-gauge
  - **4** color C (gold)
  - **2** color D (brown)
- **2** 3mm ID anodized aluminum jump rings, 18-gauge, (brass)
- toggle clasp (gold plated)

cool-tone bracelet
colors:

- color A (black)
- color B (blue)
- color C (silver)
- color D (gray)

tools

- **2** pairs of chainnose, bentnose, or flatnose pliers

4-in-1 base

[1] Close all of the color A 6mm jump rings, and open all the remaining jump rings.

[2] Slide a color C 3.9mm ring through two As, and close it **(a)**.

[3] Hold the C added in step 2 so the As flare out above the C **(b)**. Slide a C 6mm ring through two new As, then slide it down through the front of the right-hand A and up through the back of the left-hand A added in step 2, and close it **(c)**.

[4] Repeat step 3 to add the remaining As.

[5] Slide a C 3.9mm down through the front of the last right-hand A and up through the back of the last left-hand A, and close it **(d)**.

Half-Persian edging

[6] At the starting end of the 4-in-1 base, begin working on the right side of the chain. Slide a color B 6mm ring up through the back of the second A and down through the front of the first A, and close it **(e)**.

[7] Slide a B up through the back of the third A and down through the front of the second and first As, and close it **(f)**, making sure you are placing the new B behind the previous B added. Repeat this step to the end of the base.

[8] At the end of the right-hand side, slide a B through the front of the last two As, and close it **(g)**.

[9] Go back to the starting end of the base to work on the left-hand side. Slide a B up through the back of the first A and down through the front of the second A, and close it **(h)**.

[10] Slide a B up through the back of the first and second As and down through the front of the third A, and close it **(i)**, making sure you're placing the new B behind the previous B. Repeat this step for the length of the base.

[11] At the end of the left-hand side, slide a B through the back of the last two As, and close it **(j)**.

Join the edges

[12] Return to the starting end of the bracelet, and turn it over. Run your finger down the spine of As to make the Bs flip in toward the center (the position they need to be in as you join them). Slide a D 3.9mm ring down through the end B on the right side and up through the end B on the left side, and close it **(k)**.

[13] Slide a D 6mm ring down through the first and second Bs on the right side and up through the second and first Bs on the left side, and close it **(l)**.

[14] Slide a D 6mm down through the second and third Bs on the right side and up through the third and second Bs on the left side, and close it **(m)**. Continue to connect the remaining edge links.

[15] At the end of the bracelet, slide a D 3.9mm down through the last B on the right side and up through the last B on the left side, and close it **(n)**.

Add the toggle clasp

[16] Slide a C 3.9mm through the toggle ring and the D 3.9mm and C 3.9mm on one end, and close it **(o)**.

[17] Slide a C 3.9mm through the D 3.9mm and C 3.9mm on the other end, and close it.

[18] Slide a 3mm jump ring through the C 3.9mm added in step 17, and close it. Slide another 3mm jump ring through this 3mm and the toggle bar, and close it **(p)**.

Technique Tip

It's important to work with the same surface facing up for the 4-in-1 base and half-Persian edging. To make sure you're always working on the right side, mark the first 3.9mm ring with a twist tie: Fold the twist tie in half, guide the fold through the ring, and pull the twist tie ends through the fold to make a lark's head knot with the folded loop on the top surface of the chain. Then, if you drop the chain, you'll be able to figure out which surface is the top.

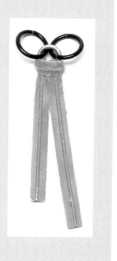

Laura Poplin

"I love the fabric-like properties of chain mail and the depth it gives finished jewelry."

Although Laura's background is in corporate sales, she has always dabbled in creative pursuits, such as knitting, sewing, and decorating. After trying several jewelry-making techniques, she found her true passion in a chain mail class. She began experimenting with many of the 1,000+ weaves, and eventually added metalwork, leather, and enameling to the mix. She enjoys the unlimited design possibilities available when techniques are combined.

Akemi
earrings

These earrings use a simple 2+2 chain pattern. Antiqued copper and amber-colored beads give them an organic, vintage feel.

materials

- Antiqued copper jump rings:
  - **36** 18-gauge 3.25mm (large)
  - **40** 20-gauge 2.75mm (small)
- 20- or 22-gauge copper sheet, approx. 2x2 in.
- **10** 4–5mm beads
- **10** antiqued copper headpins
- Pair of earring wires or post-back earring findings

tools & supplies

- **2** pairs of chainnose, bentnose, or flatnose pliers
- Jeweler's saw and blades
- Hand file set
- Drill with #67 drill bit
- Center punch
- Texture hammer
- Bench block
- Patina

a

Metalwork

[1] Follow the template to make two triangle shapes. Apply the texture and patina of your choice.

Chain mail

[2] Using 10 large rings and eight small, make a 2+2 chain (see tutorial, page 62).

[3] Using six large rings and four small, make a second 2+2 chain. Attach the shorter chain to the three middle rings of the longer chain using two small rings for each connection.

template

[4] Attach two additional large rings to the center ring of the bottom triplet using two small rings.

[5] Repeat to make a second Japanese 12-in-2 section for the other earring.

[6] Place the chain below each triangle shape and mark placement of the holes **(a)**. Using a #67 drill bit, drill five evenly spaced holes along the bottom of each triangle and one at the top of each as shown on the template. Use a file to remove any burrs and smooth the edges of the shapes.

Wirework

[7] Make 10 wrapped-loop dangles with the beads and headpins.

[8] Attach each chain mail section to a triangle using the small rings. Attach a bead dangle to each of the five bottom rings using the existing large rings **(b)**. Attach each triangle to an earring wire.

b

Japanese Variations Tutorial

The Japanese category of chain mail usually consists of layers of jump rings held together by smaller rings, although you can find many complicated variations as well. This tutorial is a basic 12-in-2 pattern; it is the basis for many more-complicated weaves. The flat surface of these weaves makes Japanese-style chain a perfect foil for leather and metal shapes.

This tutorial demonstrates the 12-in-2 weave using 16 18-gauge 3.25mm jump rings (shown in antiqued brass) and 14 20-gauge 2.75mm jump rings (silver). This technique can be adapted to connect any lengths of chain made in A and B.

The most common ring sizes used for sturdy jewelry made with this type of weave are 18-gauge 3.25mm and 20-gauge 2.75mm.

[1] Close all large rings and open all small rings. Pass an open ring through four closed rings and close it. Pass another open ring through the same four closed rings. Arrange the chain in a 2+2+2 pattern **(a)**.

[2] Add to the chain by passing a small ring through two of the previously added large rings and two new large rings. Repeat to add a second small ring through the same four large rings.

a

b

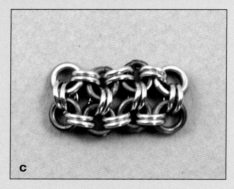

c

Continue until the chain consists of eight pairs of large rings connected to seven pairs of small rings **(b)**.

[3] Fold the chain in half. Pass a small ring through the two large rings on each end and close it. Pass an additional small ring through the same two pairs and close it. Repeat across the row until the chains are connected into a rectangle **(c)**.

Lille
bracelet

This design combines three of my favorite unconventional materials. It gives you opportunities to express your style if you'd like to vary the colors of the leather and the texture of the metal.

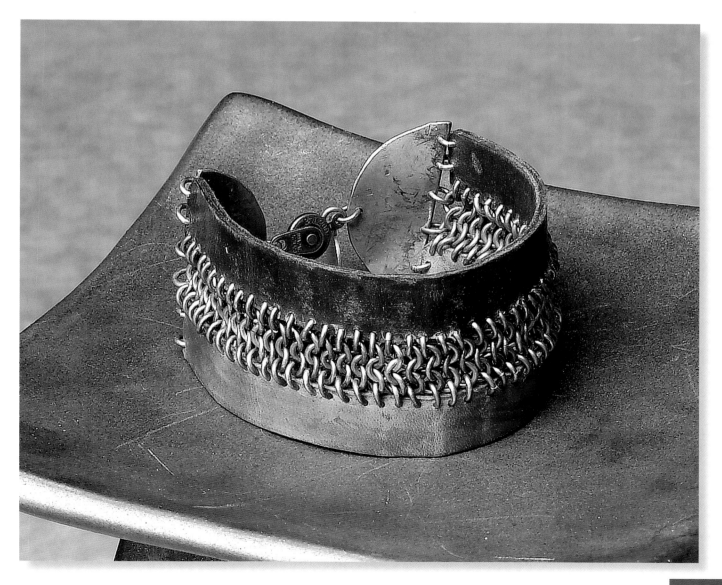

materials

bracelet 7¼ in. (18.4cm)

- Brass jump rings:
  - **130** 18-gauge 3.25mm
  - **90** 18-gauge 3mm
- **2** 5½ in. finished leather strips
- Ball-and-socket clasp
- **2** brass shapes from template

tools & supplies

- **2** pairs of chainnose, bentnose, or flatnose pliers
- Needle tool or pick
- awl
- Jeweler's saw and blades
- Hand file set
- Drill and drill bits
- Center punch
- Texture hammer
- Bench block
- Butane torch
- Solderite pad or charcoal block
- Sandpaper or sanding pads
- Polishing cloth or pads

[1] Anneal half of the brass jump rings to darken them.

Chain mail

[2] Make a 5½-in. (14 cm) single European 4-in-1 chain (tutorial, page 65) and adjust the length if necessary.

Textured sheet metal shapes

[3] Apply texture and patina to the metal shapes, and finish as desired.

[4] Drill six holes along the straight edge of each shape and one for the clasp attachment as shown on the template.

[5] Place the chain between the leather strips and use the awl to mark placement of 45 holes that will connect the chain to each leather piece.

[6] Drill the holes and use 3mm jump rings to connect the chain to the leather.

Connect

[7] Place a metal shape at one end of the bracelet and mark the hole placement on the leather. Repeat for the second end, marking two holes in each end of each leather strip.

[8] Drill the end holes **(a)**.

[9] Use 3mm jump rings to attach the metal shapes to the bracelet; attach two rings to each leather strip and two to the chain **(b)**.

[10] Use 3mm rings to attach half of the clasp at each end.

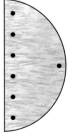

template

European 4-in-1 Tutorial

Of all the chain mail weaves, European 4-in-1 is the most versatile. When made with small rings, it feels like a wonderful fabric. Using larger rings creates a more organic look.

Close two-thirds of your rings and open the other third.

Pass an open ring through four closed rings and close it **(a)**. Place the unit of five as shown **(b)**. Pass a new open ring through the two top rings **(c)**. Add two closed rings to the open ring and close it **(d)**. Arrange the rings you just added to match the pattern set by the first five rings **(e)**. Repeat the previous step until the chain is the desired length **(f)**.

Build a second chain the same size as the first and lay them side by side **(g)**. Join the two 4-in-1 chains by passing an open ring through the inside, top two rings on each chain **(h)**. Continue by connecting the last connected pair with the next unconnected pair **(i)**. Continue connecting the two chains with single rings until the end **(j)**.

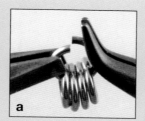

a

b

c

d

e

f

g

h

i

j

Joie de Vivre
pendant

This pendant gives you plenty of opportunities for personalization (hint—it makes a great gift). Incorporate meaningful phrases or add some birthstone crystals or favorite beads.

materials

for the chrysanthemum unit:
- Copper jump rings:
  - **55** 21-gauge ³/₃₂-in.
  - **1** 16-gauge ⁹/₃₂-in.
- Sterling silver rings:
  - **13** 21-gauge ⅛-in.

for the bail:
- **8** 18-gauge 3.25mm brass rings
- Sterling silver jump rings:
  - **8** 20-gauge 2.75mm
  - **2** 20-gauge 3.75mm
  - **2** 18-gauge ³/₁₆-in.
  - **5** 3.75mm sterling silver jump rings
- **3** pieces of sheet metal (sterling silver, copper, and brass), 20- or 22-gauge, each approx. 1x1½ in. (enough for one leaf shape)
- 14-gauge half-hard sterling silver wire, 4½ in.
- Leather cord necklace, 16–18 in.

tools & supplies
- **2** pairs of chainnose, bentnose, or flatnose pliers
- Jeweler's saw and blades
- Hand file set
- Drill and drill bits
- Center punch
- Chasing hammer
- Texture hammer
- Bench block
- Butane torch
- Paste solder
- Solderite pad or charcoal block
- Sandpaper or sanding pads
- Liver of sulfur
- Polishing cloth or pads
- Alphabet and/or design stamps
- Tumbler (optional)

Practice stamping words on a scrap piece of metal to perfect your stamping technique and ensure the words will fit.

The pendant components

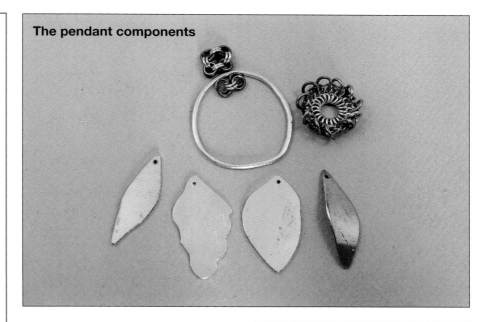

Chain mail
[1] Make one Chrysanthemum unit (tutorial, page 68) with the copper, sterling silver, and brass jump rings. Tumble-polish if desired.

Wire hoop
[2] Make a hoop from the sterling silver wire, and solder it closed. Sand and finish the join until it is smooth.

Bail
[3] Make two 2+2 chains using the 18-gauge 3.25mm brass rings and the 20-gauge 2.75mm silver rings.

[4] Lay one chain above the wire hoop and one inside it.

[5] Use four 20-gauge 3.75mm rings to connect the two chains, enclosing the hoop.

[6] Attach the Chrysanthemum unit to the bottom of the bail with two 21-gauge ³/₃₂-in. rings **(a)**.

Metal leaf shapes
[7] Trace three leaf templates (below) onto the metal sheet.

[8] Cut out the leaves and finish the edges with files and sandpaper.

[9] Drill a hole at the top of each leaf. Stamp letters, words, phrases, or designs on each leaf.

[10] Apply patina to the leaves. Sand the surfaces to create contrast with the stamped letters. Attach the leaves to the bottom of the hoop with 3.75mm jump rings. Tumble if desired. Attach the bail to the leather cord with the remaining three 3.75mm jump rings.

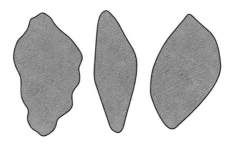

templates

Chrysanthemum Weave Tutorial

The Chrysanthemum weave is based on the European 4-in-1, which is one of the oldest, most popular weaves. The units can be attached together to make a bracelet, but unless other elements are supporting and protecting this delicate flower, it can be rather fragile. I like to make this weave using a variety of jump ring colors.

The tutorial uses these ring sizes:
55 21-gauge ³⁄₃₂ in.
1 16-gauge ⁹⁄₃₂ in.
11 18-gauge ⁵⁄₃₂ in.
13 21-gauge ⅛ in.

[1] Close 22 21-gauge ³⁄₃₂-in. rings, slide them onto the 16-gauge 5mm ring, and close the 5mm ring **(a)**. Open the remaining 22 ³⁄₃₂-in. rings.

[2] Pass an open ³⁄₃₂-in. ring through the first and second ring, and close it. Pass an open ³⁄₃₂-in. ring through the second and third ring, and close it **(b)**.

[3] Continue working in the same direction around the large ring, making sure each ring you add lies under the previous ring **(c)**.

[4] You should have 11 18-gauge ⁵⁄₃₂-in. rings, 11 21-gauge ³⁄₃₂-in. rings, and 13 21-gauge ⅛-in. rings remaining. Proceed with the next row in the same manner, except alternate 18-gauge rings and 21-gauge ⅛-in. rings **(d)**.

[5] Pass an open 21-gauge ³⁄₃₂-in. ring through two 21-gauge ⅛-in. rings from the previous row. This takes place in the middle of the 18-gauge rings and causes the flower to become three-dimensional **(e)**.

[6] Continue around to create the finished flower **(f)**.

a

b

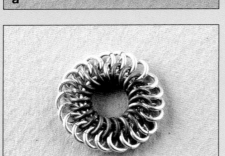

c

d

e

f

This weave requires accurate aspect ratio. If you're making jump rings, test a few before you cut an entire batch.

Clichy
pendant & earrings

The twisted wire of the Clichy pendant and earrings gives the double hoops extra dimension and provides textural contrast to the shiny Herkimer diamonds and pearls. Create one Clichy component for a pendant or two for earrings—the technique is exactly the same; you'll just change the sizes of the jump rings and beads. If you'd like a petite version of the earrings, try using only one hoop or make the hoops smaller.

materials

pendant

- Sterling silver jump rings:
  - **70** 18-gauge 3.5mm
  - **10** 18-gauge 3.25mm
  - **4** 18-gauge 6mm
  - **8** 18-gauge 3mm
- Sterling silver twisted wire, 14-gauge, 8¼ in. cut into a 5¼-in. and a 3-in. piece
- **7** 6mm Herkimer diamond beads
- **9** 6mm pearls
- **16** antiqued 24-gauge sterling silver headpins
- Leather cord necklace

earrings

- Sterling silver jump rings:
  - **162** 20-gauge 2.75mm
  - **20** 18-gauge 3mm
- 16-gauge twisted wire, 11 in. cut into two 5-in. and two 3-in. pieces
- **18** 4mm Herkimer diamond or smoky quartz beads
- **18** 24-gauge silver headpins
- **30** 3mm pearls
- Pair of earring wires

tools

- **2** pairs of chainnose, bentnose, or flatnose pliers
- Butane torch
- Paste solder
- Solderite pad or charcoal block
- Sandpaper or sanding pads
- Liver of sulfur
- Polishing cloth or pads
- Bezel or ring mandrel
- Oval bracelet mandrel
- Rawhide mallet

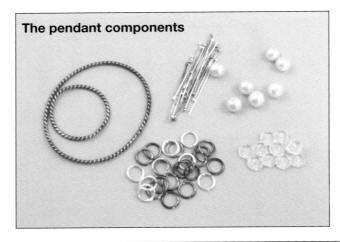

The pendant components

A Herkimer diamond is a somewhat rare quartz crystal with a point at each end. Any clear, faceted gemstone is a good substitute.

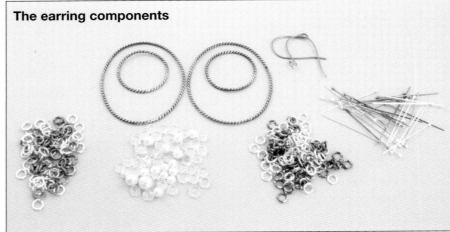

The earring components

a

b

Hoop sets

[1] Form each piece of twisted wire into a hoop and solder the ends together.

[2] Gently shape the small hoop on a bezel or ring mandrel using a rawhide mallet.

[3] Use an oval bracelet mandrel to shape the larger hoop in the same way **(a)**.

[4] Antique the hoops, headpins, jump rings, and earring wires; buff the hoops with a polishing cloth or sandpaper to accent the design; and tumble-polish if desired.

Chain mail and dangles

[5] Working with 3.5mm jump rings for a pendant or 2.75mm jump rings for earrings, attach 10 rings to the small hoop.

[6] Add two rows as explained in the European 4-in-1 Triangle Tutorial (page 72), attaching a Herkimer diamond bead dangle to each jump ring in the second row before closing it.

[7] Add a ring with a bead on each side.

[8] Add 13 jump rings to the large hoop and complete in the same way as the small hoop.

[9] On the last row, add a wrapped-loop pearl dangle to each ring before closing it. Add a ring with a pearl dangle on each side of the triangle **(b)**.

Make two sets of hoop components for earrings.

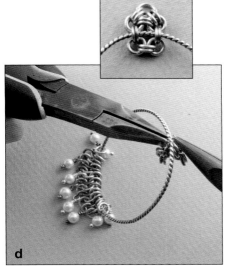

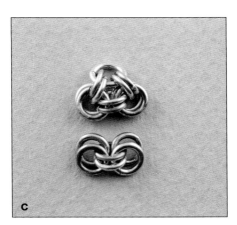

c

d

e

Chain mail bail

The bail is based on a variation of the Japanese 12-in-2 weave (see tutorial on page 62).

[10] For earrings: Using 18-gauge, 3mm (large) and 20-gauge, 2.75mm (small) rings, make a 2+2+2+2+2 chain. Connect the end pairs with a pair of small rings to form a triangle **(c, top)**. Make a 2+2+2 chain **(c, bottom)**.

[11] Place the chain triangle above the wire hoop and the straight chain inside it. Use four small rings to connect the two chains, enclosing the hoop **(d)**.

[12] Attach the small hoop to the bottom of the straight chain using four 20-gauge 2.75mm rings **(e)**. Make a second earring.

[13] For a pendant: Using 18-gauge, 3.25mm and 18-gauge, 3mm rings, make two 2+2 chains and connect them to make a square.

[14] Attach the bottom of the square to the two hoops using four 3.25mm rings. At the top, attach the square to the leather cord using four 6mm rings.

European 4-in-1 Triangle Tutorial

Attach an odd number of closed rings to a scrap wire and twist the wire closed **(a)**. (If your project calls for the triangle to end on a wire shape, you can build it on that wire.)

Pass an open ring through the first two rings and close. Pass an open ring through the third and second ring **(b)** and close. Pass an open ring through the fourth and third ring and close. Add one ring at a time in the same way until you reach the end of the row **(c)**.

Repeat the previous step with each row until the last row has only one ring **(d)**. A finished triangle **(e)**.

a

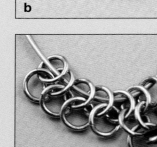

b

c

d

e

Basics & more

- Tools
- Jump rings
- Soldering
- Finishing
- Jewelry-making techniques

Confused about aspect ratio? Wondering how to make your own jump rings? Need a refresher on making a perfect wrapped loop? Not sure about soldering? You'll find everything you need to know in this comprehensive Basics section.

Beyond the basics, Vanessa Walilko and Anne Mitchell provide commentary on chain mail standards and practices, and on using aspect ratio to control the fit of a piece.

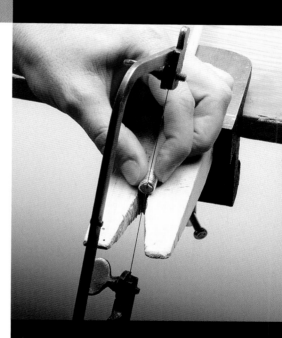

Tools

One of the best things about making chain mail jewelry is the relatively few tools it requires. You absolutely must have two pairs of pliers and a pair of wire cutters. The rest of the tools here have to do with specialty techniques or finishing options.

Pliers

When purchasing pliers, inspect the jaws to see that they are smooth and even, look for a solid joint with a little give or wiggle, and try out the handle. When you spend a lot of time with tools in your hand, comfort is important. Here are some of the basic types of pliers and what they do. For chain mail, you'll choose two pairs (either the same type or two different styles) from the first four pliers in the list.

Chainnose pliers have flat inner jaws, great for gripping jump rings and opening and closing loops.

Flatnose pliers can be used in the same manner as chainnose, but their flat outer jaws make it easier to make sharper bends in the wire.

Bentnose pliers are similar to chainnose pliers, but they have a slight bend near the tips. They are often easier to manipulate than straight chainnose pliers are, especially in tight spaces like a chain mail weave.

Nylon-jaw pliers feature replaceable nylon lining on the jaws, which protects wire and jump rings from marks left by tools. These are particularly useful with jump rings that have a thin coating of color that could easily scratch off, such as niobium.

Roundnose pliers are critical for making loops. These pliers have conical jaws.

Cutters

Side cutters are the most common type of cutters. As the name implies, these cutters have blades that are parallel to their handles. Some side cutters have blades that are tilted slightly upward. These are useful because they can cut wire from several angles. Side cutters produce a flush cut on one side and a pinched cut on the other. For jump rings, the pinched side must be cut a second time to make it flush so the jump ring can close properly.

Flush cutters leave less of a bevel, and super-flush or ultra-flush cutters produce a flatter cut and require even less energy to use. However, in exchange for their tremendous cutting ability, super-flush cutters lose strength, so you can use them only for wire finer than 18-gauge.

Jeweler's saws have two parts: an adjustable U-shaped frame with a handle, and a blade. You can use a variety of different blade sizes or thicknesses in the saw; use stronger blades for thicker metal. Use saws to cut shapes from metal and saw through coils to make jump rings.

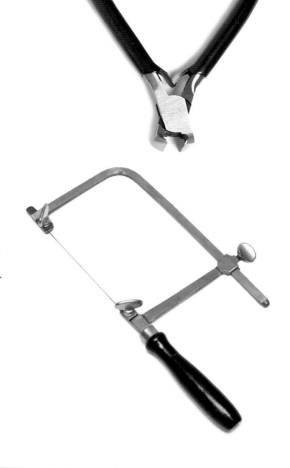

Dowels and mandrels

Dowels are cylindrical rods, frequently made of wood, that jewelry makers use for shaping wire into jump rings and coils. **Mandrels** are made of steel, plastic, or wood, and have a smooth or stepped taper, so that rings and coils can be easily measured and removed.

Jewelry makers are frequently creative with mandrels and often use other tools, like punches or knitting needles, as mandrels.

Torches

Torches are necessary for annealing and soldering wire components and jump rings. They differ greatly in price range, temperature, and fuel. For our purposes, a simple butane torch is adequate for soldering jump rings.

Files

Metal **files** are used to refine and shape the edges of metal and wire surfaces.

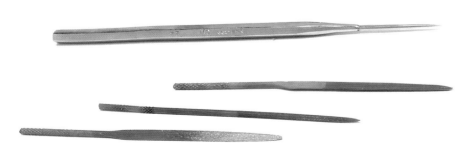

Jump Ring Metals

Gold and silver are the most traditional choices for jump rings, but jump rings are also made from brass, copper, steel, and niobium.

Silver

There are four common silver options: fine silver, sterling silver, Argentium sterling silver, and silver plated. Of these, **fine silver** is the purest, composed almost entirely of silver. Because fine silver is soft, it is not ideal for chain mail.

Sterling silver and Argentium sterling have been alloyed with other metals for additional strength. **Sterling silver** has long been the material of choice for jewelry makers, since it is strong and malleable. Sterling silver is 92.5% fine silver with 7.5% copper and other metals—thus the .925 stamp on sterling. The drawback to sterling is that its small copper content makes it oxidize at a faster rate than fine silver, so it tends to tarnish quickly.

Argentium sterling is an alloy that substitutes a higher germanium content for the copper to avoid the tarnishing problem while retaining strength. Argentium sterling is considered a great technological advancement in silver, having the best qualities of sterling without its oxidation rate. It is a bit stiffer than sterling to work with. Both are excellent materials for jump rings.

Silver-plated wire is frequently found in beading stores and craft shops. This wire is formed by layering sterling silver over a copper or brass core. If the ends are exposed (as on wrapped loops), or the wire is hammered, the core will show. For that reason, many jewelry makers avoid using silver-plated wire.

Gold

Gold wire is sold in different karat weights, tempers, and even colors. Pure, 24k gold is very soft to work with,

while 14k gold is a ⁷/₁₂-gold alloy and is stronger. Gold-filled wire is an economical choice at a fraction of the cost of 14k-gold wire. Contrary to its name, gold-filled wire is actually gold overlay. A thin layer of 14k gold is heat- and pressure-bonded to a brass core. The layer of pure gold makes the wire tarnish-resistant, and it should be cared for just like the expensive version. Buff gold-filled wire with a soft, clean cloth (such as flannel) and store it in a dry place. Placing tissue paper around the gold-filled wire will minimize exposure to humidity and prevent scratching while it's being stored. Both 14k gold and gold-filled are good choices for jump rings and chain mail.

Niobium

Niobium has the same strength as half-hard sterling silver, but it's about 20 percent lighter. One benefit of niobium is that it's hypoallergenic. Many people who can't wear silver or other common jewelry metals wear niobium with no negative effects.

Niobium gets its color from an anodizing process, which coats the surface of the metal with an oxide layer. This is accomplished with an electric charge. The voltage of the charge determines the thickness of the oxide layer, which in turn determines the color. Anodizing is used to prepare many metals for dyeing, because the porous oxide layer allows dye to enter.

The same process turns titanium and niobium a range of colors without the use of dyes.

The colored surface of anodized niobium is just that—on the surface. The layer of color is easily scratched, exposing the natural silver color of the niobium. Coating pliers with Tool Magic or painter's tape will help protect niobium jump rings during chain mail assembly.

Making and Using Jump Rings

Coiling jump rings by hand

Select a wooden dowel or mandrel with a diameter that matches the inside diameter of the jump rings you want to make. Drill a hole through one end of the dowel. Insert the end of the wire into the hole, and coil the wire around the dowel.

Cut the wire that anchors the coil. If you will be using wire cutters to cut the coil into jump rings, remove the coil from the dowel. If you will be using a jeweler's saw, slide the coil to the opposite end of the dowel.

Making jump rings with a jump ring maker

1 If you have a jump ring maker or other tool, follow the manufacturer's instructions to make your coil.
2 Following the manufacturer's instructions, secure the coil in the holding device.
3 Cut the jump rings, following the manufacturer's instructions.

Cutting jump rings using wire cutters

1 Holding the flush-cut edge of your cutters at a right angle to the coil, trim the straight wire tail from each end of the coil.
2 Slightly separate the first ring from the coil. Holding the flush-cut edge of your cutters at a right angle to the coil, cut where the wire completes the first ring.

If you use diagonal wire cutters, one end of your ring will be flush and the other end will be pointed. To flush-cut the pointed end, flip your cutters over to the flush-cut side, and cut again so that both cuts are flush. Then, flush-cut the end of the coil to start the next ring. There will be some wire waste, so make a few extra coils to make up for it.

Cutting jump rings using a jeweler's saw

Secure the dowel against the V notch in your bench pin, and use a jeweler's saw with a 2/0 blade to cut a shallow, vertical slot at the end of the dowel to guide your blade as you cut the coil.

Hold the coil and dowel with your nondominant hand. Saw through the top of the coil, feeding it toward the slot in the dowel. Be careful not to cut the jump rings in half.

Opening and closing a jump ring

1 Hold the jump ring with two pairs of pliers, such as chainnose, flatnose, or bentnose. To open the jump ring, bring one pair of pliers toward you, and push the other pair away from you. Do not pull the jump ring open sideways.
2 To close the jump ring, reverse the direction of the pliers to bring the ends of the jump ring back together. Because jump rings (especially those used in chain mail) tend to spring back, you may find it helpful to bring the tips of the ring a bit past the closed position and then bring them back together.

Jump ring sizes

The inside diameter (ID) of a jump ring is measured by the size of the mandrel used to make it. Some jump ring manufacturers use mandrels that are measured in fractional inches (such as $1/8$ in.), while others use mandrels measured in millimeters, which come in quarter-millimeter increments. Likewise, some of the artists in this book have listed their materials in inches, and others specify millimeters. When you are shopping for jump rings to make a project, this can be confusing. For instance, if the project you're working on calls for $15/64$-in. jump rings and the vendor you're buying from sells them in fractional inches, you're good to go. But what if the ones you're purchasing are measured in millimeters?

This chart will help you convert from one measurement to the other.

Ring Size in Fractional Inches	Ring Size in Millimeters
$3/32$ in.	2.5mm
$1/8$ in.	3.25mm
$9/64$ in.	3.5mm
$5/32$ in.	4.0mm
$3/16$ in.	4.75mm
$7/32$ in.	5.5mm
$15/64$ in.	6.0mm
$11/32$ in.	8.75mm
$3/8$ in.	9.5mm
$1/2$ in.	13.0mm

Soldering

Solder is a metal alloy that is used to join two pieces of metal. You can buy solder as wire, paste, or sheet. Solder is available in different grades, ranging from extra hard to extra easy. The harder the solder, the slower it melts. For that reason, if there is more than one solder join in a piece, solder the first one using hard solder, the second using medium solder, and the third using easy solder.

Flux is available as a liquid powder or paste, and is used to coat a surface before solder is applied. Flux helps prevent oxides from forming on the metal when it is heated, which helps solder flow properly.

A *torch* is used to heat the solder and the pieces you wish to join.

Always use a fire-resistant surface, like a *fire brick* or *charcoal block*, and work in a well-ventilated area.

Water is used for quenching and rinsing the pieces. Fill two heat-resistant bowls: one to quench the piece after soldering, and the other to rinse off the pickle.

A *solder pick* is an awl-like tool with a metal tip and an insulated handle (such as wood) used to move and pick up solder. Solder doesn't stick to the metals used in solder picks, like steel, titanium, and tungsten carbide.

Pickle cleans metal and dissolves the flux after the piece is fired. It is slightly acidic, so use it in a well-ventilated area, and take care to keep it off clothes, skin, and other surfaces.

Use *copper tongs* with pickle, as stainless steel will cause a copper plating of other metals in the pickle.

A *warming pot* can be used to keep pickle at a warmer temperature, which makes it work more quickly.

Prepare the join

All metal surfaces must be clean in order for solder to flow. Clean metal by sanding it with 400-grit sandpaper and rinsing it. The surfaces must be in complete contact with each other in order for the solder to join them—solder will not fill holes or gaps.

Flux and heat

Flux the area to be soldered to prevent oxidation. You can apply flux with a dropper or paint it on with a brush (**a**). Place the solder on the join and heat the entire piece, not just the solder (**b**). Keep the torch moving in a circular motion. Solder will flow toward the source of the heat, so once the solder begins to flow you can use your torch to direct it where you want it to go. When the solder flows, you'll see a flash of silver and it will move into the join. When this happens, immediately remove the heat.

Pickle and rinse

Once the solder flows, quench the piece in water, and place it in a pickle solution to remove oxidation and flux residue until it is clean and white (for silver). Rinse the piece in clean water.

Annealing

The temper of wire is its hardness, or malleability. Silver and gold wires can be purchased at different levels of hardness, such as dead-soft, half-hard, or full-hard. When working with metal, you want it to be pliable enough to manipulate, yet strong enough to hold its shape. Working with wire strengthens it; this is called work-hardening. Additional strength comes with hammering after you've formed your shape. The trick is to use wire that is soft enough to work with but becomes hard enough to hold the final shape. You likely will want to work with half-hard wire the majority of the time. When connecting elements with double-wrapped loops, the act of wrapping the loops is enough manipulation to fully work-harden the wire so it is at its maximum strength. If you used full-hard wire, it could be too difficult to manipulate. If you use dead-soft wire, it could only become half-hard after wrapping, so it would not maintain its shape as well.

Annealing is the process of heating work-hardened metal until it softens enough to be malleable. Put your metal on a fire-resistant surface, and heat the metal with a torch until it glows a subtle pink. Immediately remove the heat when you see the color, or you'll burn or melt the metal. Dim or turn off the lights to help you see this color change. To finish, quench the metal in water and put it in warm pickle to remove any oxides.

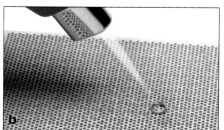

Standards and Practices in Chain Mail—Vanessa Walilko

Jewelry makers are eager for information, tips, and patterns that will help them create successful chain mail pieces. My hope is that this review of standards for chain mail will help you make beautiful jewelry.

Finding closure

Getting a good closure on your rings is one of the most important aspects of successful chain mail jewelry and one of the hardest to master. A good closure shows that you care about making sure that every ring is securely attached to the piece. A hair's breadth of a gap in your ring might not seem like a big deal. But if all of your rings have that much of an opening, chances are that the openings will at some point line up and the rings will come apart.

If you're not sure how your closures measure up, hold the ring up to the light. If light shines through the gap, you'll need to adjust to line up the ends of the wire perfectly. No light means you're on the way to making your closure just right. **Photo a** shows a good closure. The ends of the wire are lined up and totally flush.

Troubleshooting

Most inadequate closures fall into one of three camps, but thankfully there's an easy way to fix each one once identified.

The most common problem is when the gap in the ring is clearly visible **(b)**. To get a better closure, press the ends of the ring inward as you twist it closed.

Photo c shows an overbite—one end of the ring is higher than the other. This means that you're twisting the ring with unequal pressure. Loosen up your grip on your pliers, and be mindful of pressing in the ends of the ring with equal force.

A more subtle problem occurs when the edges of the ring curve instead of lying flat **(d)**. To fix this problem, make sure your pliers aren't angled while twisting them back and forth.

Aside from looking more professional, perfect closures ensure that your jewelry pieces are comfortable. If you're an aspiring jewelry designer, you don't want to be known as the artist who makes pieces that scratch!

Get a grip

A good grip on your jump rings reduces the chances of marring them. The plier edges can dig into the rings as you twist them open, leaving visible nicks in the surface **(e)**. The result is a piece that looks like it's been poorly cared for before it's even been worn. The effects are more visible on a larger ring since you need more force to twist it open.

Plier position is also important in getting a good grip. You want to cover a good portion of the ring with your pliers to get the torque necessary for effective twisting. With the tips of the pliers angled toward the opening, grip the ring at what would be the 10 o'clock and 2 o'clock positions of a clock face **(f)**.

a

b

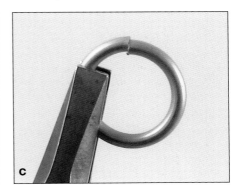
c

d

e

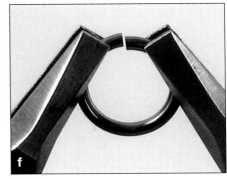
f

Reversible Chain Reaction
bracelet by Vanessa Walilko

One of the best ways to get a good grip is to coat the jaws of your pliers. Tool Magic is the most effective coating, though tape can also work wonders. I usually wrap a 3-in. (7.6cm) length of masking tape tightly around the tips of my pliers, cutting off any extra tape with scissors. In either case, understand that the coatings are temporary and will have to be replaced when they get too worn to provide adequate grip.

Gauging your rings

As you work on chain mail projects, it's important to know that there are two wire gauge systems: the American Wire Gauge (AWG) and the Standard Wire Gauge (SWG) (see table, p. 85). In the United States, the American Wire Gauge (AWG) scale, also known as the Brown & Sharpe (B&S) gauge, is most commonly used to measure precious metals and the Standard Wire Gauge system is generally used for base metals, though it's not a hard-and-fast rule. Why does this matter? If a pattern was designed with rings in AWG, you might not be able to complete the weave if you use SWG rings. If you're ever in doubt, ask the supplier about the diameter of the wire to make sure you'll be able to use the rings for your intended project.

Aspect ratio

Aspect ratio is a numerical description of the diameter of the wire used to make the ring compared to the inner diameter of the ring. It's important to understand if you're trying to make a specific weave but want to use a different size ring than what the instructions call for. If your rings are larger and/or made of thinner wire, the weave may not hold its shape. On the other hand, if the rings are smaller and/or made of thicker wire, you may not be able to fit the rings together at all in the intended pattern. While many jump rings are sold with the inner diameter listed in millimeters, the diameter of the wire gauge usually isn't specified. Refer to the AWG/SWG chart to help you get started on figuring out aspect ratio. For more about aspect ratio see page 83.

Know your weaves

There are several families of chain mail weaves, such as European, Persian, and Japanese. If you're not familiar with the characteristics of the weave families, visit mailleartisans.org, the website of the Maille Artisans International League. With well over 1,000 weaves and variations catalogued, the site offers lots of information and inspiration.

Control the Fit of Your Chain Mail Weave—Anne Mitchell

Aspect ratio (AR) sounds intimidating because, let's face it, it's math. But conquer this one simple formula, and you'll have complete control over the density of your chain mail work. Do you want an open and airy version of a Byzantine link, or do you like the look of a tightly woven chain? The following information will guide you on the correct choice of jump rings.

The basic formula

Essentially, calculating aspect ratio means figuring out how many jump rings each jump ring can comfortably hold. The math is based on the relationship between the ring's inside diameter (ID) and the thickness of the wire that makes the ring.

Why use a jump ring's ID in the formula instead of its outside diameter (OD)? Because, as seen below, a 5.5mm ID jump ring will have the same ID whether it's made of 16- or 20-gauge wire, but its OD will be different.

5.5 mm ID

So, here's the formula to find AR:

$$ID \div gauge = AR$$

Basic math: If ID and gauge are equal, the ratio is 1, which means that one jump ring threaded through a second would completely fill the second jump ring. The greater the AR, the more space there is for additional rings, so the weave is looser.

Notes about ID and gauge

If you're buying premade jump rings, the supplier will tell you the ID and gauge of your jump rings.

The ID is usually given in millimeters. But there's a caveat, called "springback." Most manufacturers base ID on the size of the mandrel that the wire was coiled around when the jump rings were made. But when that coil is cut into jump rings, the rings tend to "spring back" slightly, so the actual ID of the rings is slightly larger than the mandrel's diameter.

The degree of springback varies with the hardness of the wire. The most reliable way to calculate your ID: Use digital calipers to measure the ID of 10–15 rings from your stash and find the average.

Convert before you calculate

Before you can plug numbers into the AR formula, convert the ID and gauge to the same measuring system. I convert both into inches, but metric works just as well. The key conversion equivalent is:

$$1mm = 0.0394 \text{ in.}$$

To find the inch measurement for your wire gauge, measure the wire with digital calipers or consult a handy chart (page 82).

For example

To find the AR of a 5mm ID, 16-gauge jump ring, first convert to inches:

5mm ID = (5 x .0394) = 0.197 in.

16-gauge wire = 0.051 in.

Plug these numbers into the basic formula: ID ÷ gauge = AR:

0.197 ÷ 0.051 = 3.86

The AR of a 5mm ID, 16-gauge jump ring is 3.86.

AR and chain mail patterns

Many chain mail patterns require a basic understanding of AR. One of the most well known is the Jens Pind. When making a Jens Pind chain I use 6mm ID, 12-gauge jump rings. So:

0.236 ÷ 0.081 = 2.91 AR

This is a tight AR. Each link has to hold three rings snugly with a minimum of movement. If the rings are too loose, the pattern won't hold. If the rings are too small, the pattern will be too stiff, if it works at all.

What Difference Does It Make?

The following chain samples with different ARs show how ID and gauge can help you determine which jump rings to use.

Byzantine Link

Inside diameter	÷ Gauge	= AR	Result	Sample
4mm (0.157 in.)	18 (0.040 in.)	3.93	Slightly open; holds pattern well	
	16 (0.051 in.)	3.08	Too tight; no movement	
5mm (0.197 in.)	16 (0.051 in.)	3.86	Slightly open; holds pattern well	
5.5mm (0.217 in.)	17 (0.045 in.)	4.82	Very open; will not hold pattern	
	16 (0.051 in.)	4.25	Very open; holds pattern	

Full Persian (Foxtail) Link

Inside diameter	÷ Gauge	= AR	Result	Sample
5.5mm (0.217 in.)	18 (0.040 in.)	5.43	Tight weave; holds pattern well	
	17 (0.045 in.)	4.82	More open, but still holds pattern	
6.5mm (0.256 in.)	18 (0.040 in.)	6.40	Even more open and holding pattern	
7.5mm (0.296 in.)	16 (0.051 in.)	5.80	Tight weave; holds pattern well	
10mm (0.394 in.)		7.73	Too open to hold pattern	

Gauge	AWG Measurements		SWG Measurements	
24	0.02 in.	0.508mm	0.022 in.	0.558mm
22	0.025 in.	0.635mm	0.028 in.	0.711mm
21	0.029 in.	0.736mm	0.032 in.	0.812mm
20	0.032 in.	0.812mm	0.036 in.	0.914mm
19	0.036 in.	0.914mm	0.04 in.	1.016mm
18	0.04 in.	1.016mm	0.048 in.	1.219mm
17	0.045 in.	1.143mm	0.056 in.	1.422mm
16	0.051 in.	1.295mm	0.064 in.	1.625mm
14	0.064 in.	1.625mm	0.08 in.	2.03mm
12	0.08 in.	2.032mm	0.104 in.	2.641mm

Resizing Rings

Let's say you've found a density that you like for a pattern, like my 2.91 AR for the Jens Pind. What if I want to make the chain using 18-gauge instead of 12-gauge jump rings? To find the jump ring size needed, just multiply rather than divide.

AR x gauge = ID

Multiply AR (2.91) by the thickness of the 18-gauge wire (0.040 in.) and get 0.116 in., or roughly 3mm ID jump rings. (For an fractional inch/metric jump ring conversion chart, see page 79.)

Beyond Chain
by Anne Mitchell

Finishing

Tumble-polishing

Place stainless steel shot into the tumbler's barrel. Although you can use any shape of steel shot, a combination of shapes works best; the various shapes polish crevices and contours differently, ensuring an even polish.

Pour in enough water to cover the shot, and add a few drops of burnishing compound. Place your jewelry in the tumbler, and seal the barrel. Turn on the tumbler, and let it run for two hours or more. Pour the contents of the tumbler into a sieve over a sink, and rinse. Remove your jewelry, and dry it. Dry the shot before storing it.

Adding patina (darkening metal) with liver of sulfur

Polish your piece before adding patina. (If you tumble-polish your piece after patinating, reserve the used shot for future patinated pieces; the liver of sulfur residue will contaminate non-patinated pieces.) Oil and dirt on the piece can affect the patina, so clean the metal with degreasing soap first.

Prepare a liver of sulfur solution according to the manufacturer's instructions. Dip the metal in the solution for a few seconds, and then rinse the metal in cool water to stop the chemical reaction.

For a darker patina, continue to dip and rinse the metal. Use a brass brush with soapy water to remove or modify the patina. By using different temperatures and amounts of water to make the solution, you can achieve different colors of patina; experiment to find the result you prefer.

Jewelry-Making Techniques

Folded crimp

1 Position the crimp bead in the notch closest to the crimping pliers' handle.
2 Separate the wires and firmly squeeze the crimp.
3 Move the crimp into the notch at the pliers' tip and hold the crimp as shown. Squeeze the crimp bead, folding it in half at the indentation. Test that the folded crimp is secure.

Wrapped loop

1 Make sure you have at least 1¼ in. (3.2cm) of wire above the bead. With the tip of your chainnose pliers, grasp the wire directly above the bead. Bend the wire (above the pliers) into a right angle.
2 Using roundnose pliers, position the jaws in the bend.
3 Bring the wire over the top jaw of the roundnose pliers.

4 Reposition the pliers' lower jaw snugly into the loop. Curve the wire downward around the bottom of the roundnose pliers. This is the first half of a wrapped loop.
5 Position the chainnose pliers' jaws across the loop.
6 Wrap the wire around the wire stem, covering the stem between the loop and the top bead. Trim the excess wire and press the cut end close to the wraps with chainnose pliers.

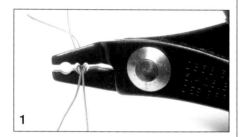

1

1

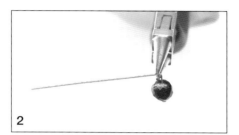

2

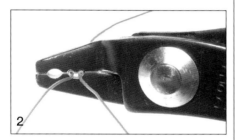

2

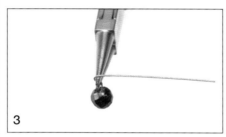

3

4

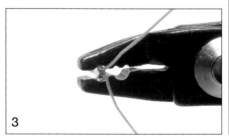

3

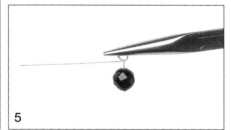

5

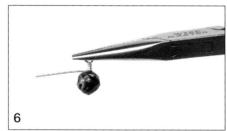

6

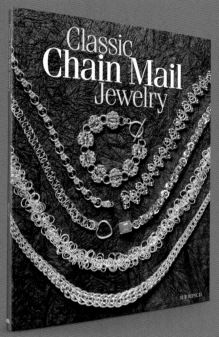
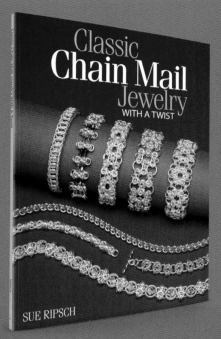
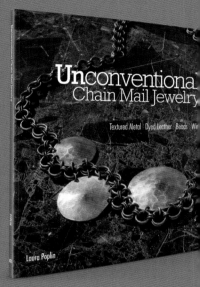